MW00996915

ARRACOURT 1944

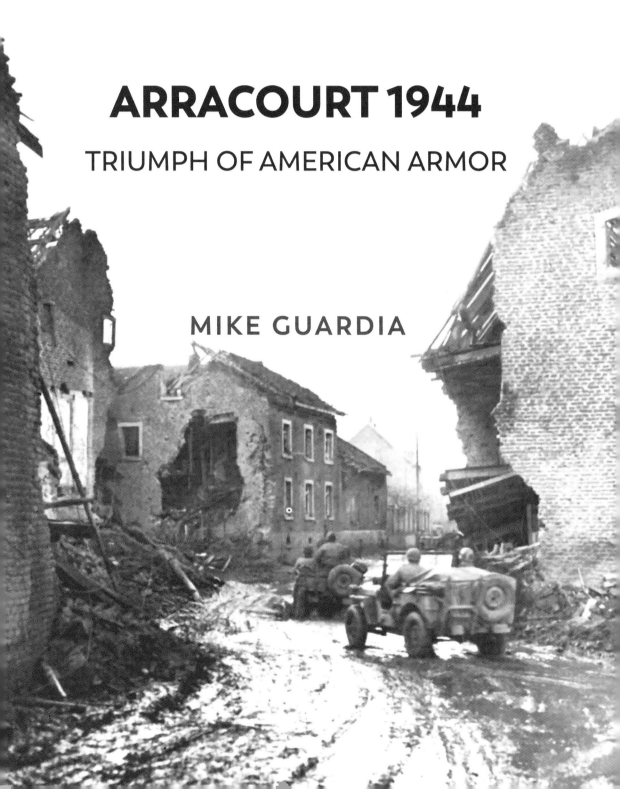

C CASEMATE | ILLUSTRATED

ARRACOURT 1944

TRIUMPH OF AMERICAN ARMOR

MIKE GUARDIA

CASEMATE | ILLUSTRATED

For Mom, Dad, Marie, and Melanie

CIS0023

Print Edition: ISBN 978-1-63624-032-9
Digital Edition: ISBN 978-1-63624-033-6

© 2022 Mike Guardia

All rights reserved. No part of this book may be reproduced or transmitted in any form or by any means, electronic or mechanical including photocopying, recording or by any information storage and retrieval system, without permission from the publisher in writing.

Design by Battlefield Design
Profiles by Paul Hewitt, Battlefield Design
Printed and bound by in the Czech Republic by FINIDR, s.r.o.

CASEMATE PUBLISHERS (US)
Telephone (610) 853-9131
Fax (610) 853-9146
Email: casemate@casematepublishers.com
www.casematepublishers.com

CASEMATE PUBLISHERS (UK)
Telephone (01865) 241249
Email: casemate-uk@casematepublishers.co.uk
www.casematepublishers.co.uk

All photos contained in this book are derived from archival sources, including the US National Archives and Records Administration, Library of Congress, Bundesarchiv, and the US Military History Institute, unless otherwise noted.

Title page: 4th Armored Division Jeeps drive through the town of Dieuze.
Contents page map: The battle of Arracourt, September 25–29, 1944. (From the U.S. Army official history, *The Lorraine Campaign*)
Contents page image: A knocked-out Panther near La Chapelle on August 2, 1944. Throughout August, there were several small-scale firefights between German and American tanks.

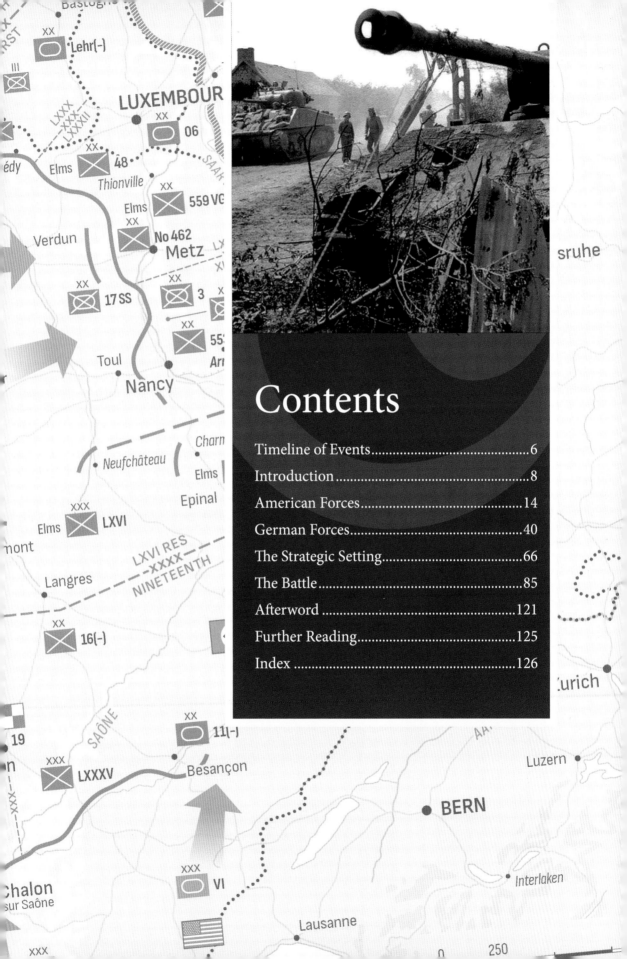

Contents

Timeline of Events...6

Introduction...8

American Forces...14

German Forces...40

The Strategic Setting......................................66

The Battle...85

Afterword..121

Further Reading..125

Index..126

Timeline of Events

The battle of Arracourt was nearly five years in the making. After hostilities began in the fall of 1939, Nazi Germany occupied France and the Low Countries within a matter of months. America entered the war in December 1941 following the attack on Pearl Harbor, but American forces did not arrive in Europe until 1943 with the invasion of Italy. As Allied forces closed in on the borders of the Reich, Hitler put the best of his remaining panzer forces along the Franco-German border, ready to stop the incoming Allied armor at any cost.

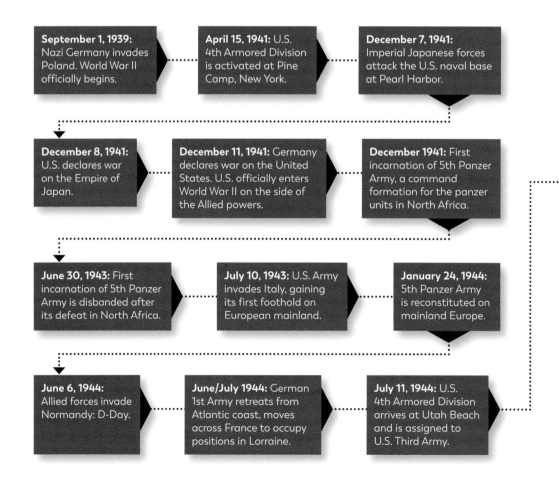

September 1, 1939: Nazi Germany invades Poland. World War II officially begins.

April 15, 1941: U.S. 4th Armored Division is activated at Pine Camp, New York.

December 7, 1941: Imperial Japanese forces attack the U.S. naval base at Pearl Harbor.

December 8, 1941: U.S. declares war on the Empire of Japan.

December 11, 1941: Germany declares war on the United States. U.S. officially enters World War II on the side of the Allied powers.

December 1941: First incarnation of 5th Panzer Army, a command formation for the panzer units in North Africa.

June 30, 1943: First incarnation of 5th Panzer Army is disbanded after its defeat in North Africa.

July 10, 1943: U.S. Army invades Italy, gaining its first foothold on European mainland.

January 24, 1944: 5th Panzer Army is reconstituted on mainland Europe.

June 6, 1944: Allied forces invade Normandy: D-Day.

June/July 1944: German 1st Army retreats from Atlantic coast, moves across France to occupy positions in Lorraine.

July 11, 1944: U.S. 4th Armored Division arrives at Utah Beach and is assigned to U.S. Third Army.

An M4 Sherman fires on an enemy stronghold near Arracourt.

July/August 1944: U.S. Third Army under General George Patton races across France.

August 15, 1944: Operation *Dragoon*, the invasion of southern France, begins.

September 1944: Hitler devises the Vosges panzer offensive, an armored counterattack to stop Patton's Third Army from reaching the River Saar and the western border of Germany.

September 1944: 111th and 113th Panzer Brigades are activated as the Allies close in on Arracourt.

September 8, 1944: First tank skirmishes in Lorraine begin.

September 10–14, 1944: 4th Armored Division begins drive into Moselle River region.

September 15, 1944: 4th Armored Division makes contact with 15th Panzergrenadier Division at Lunéville.

September 15–18, 1944: 4th Armored Division fights through German positions in and around Lunéville.

September 19, 1944: American forces enter Arracourt.

September 20, 1944: 111th Panzer Brigade attacks Combat Command A of 4th Armored Division.

September 22, 1944: 111th and 113th Panzer Brigades, assisted by panzergrenadiers, attack 37th Tank Battalion.

September 27/28, 1944: German panzergrenadiers clash with 10th Armored Infantry Battalion over control of Hill 265.

September 29, 1944: German 5th Panzer Army makes one final attempt towards Arracourt before being decimated by the 4th Armored Division.

September 30, 1944: The battered 5th Panzer Army suspends its operations at Arracourt, begins withdrawal towards the German frontier.

Introduction

September 1944: with the Allies closing in on the Rhine, Adolf Hitler orders a counterattack on General Patton's Third Army in France. Near the small town of Arracourt, elements of the U.S. 4th Armored Division meet the grizzled veterans of the German 1st Army and 5th Panzer Army in combat.

Atop their M4 Shermans, American tank crews squared off against the technologically superior Panzer IV and Panther tanks of the Wehrmacht. Yet through a combination of superior tactics, leadership, teamwork, and small-unit initiative, the outnumbered American forces won a decisive victory against the German 1st Army and 5th Panzer Army.

British forces come ashore at Normandy, June 1944. Note that the British are using an armored vehicle based upon an M4 Sherman chassis. As one of the biggest recipients of Lend-Lease equipment, British and Commonwealth forces used a variety of M3- and M4-based vehicles.

Indeed, of the 262 tanks and mobile assault guns fielded by German forces, 200 were damaged or destroyed by enemy fire. The Americans, by contrast, lost only 48 tanks. Following the collapse of the German counterattack at Arracourt, General Patton's Third Army found itself within striking distance of the Third Reich's borderlands.

The battle of Arracourt was the U.S. Army's largest tank battle until the Ardennes offensive in December 1944. It helped pave the way for the final Allied assault into Germany, and showed how tactical ingenuity and adaptive leadership can overcome an enemy's superior size or technological strength. *Arracourt 1944* provides an illustrative look at how the Wehrmacht and the U.S. Army fought each other in one of the most signature battles in modern history.

*

World War II was a conflict more than 20 years in the making. Emerging from their defeat in World War I (and the crippling terms of the Treaty of Versailles), Germany's Weimar Republic struggled to cope with the post-war devastation. From amidst the chaos and economic hardship, however, there emerged a young firebrand named Adolf Hitler—the leader of the National Socialist German Workers' (Nazi) Party. Rising to power in 1933, Hitler and his Nazi acolytes quickly turned the Weimar Republic into a single-party dictatorship. Under the banner of the "Third Reich," Hitler cast aside the terms of Versailles and rearmed the German military at an alarming rate. After annexing Austria and the Sudetenland (Czechoslovakia), Germany initiated World War II on September 1, 1939, invading Poland in the opening rounds of what would become the "blitzkrieg" campaign.

Of the towed howitzers used in the ETO, the M2-series 105mm howitzers were amongst the most ubiquitous. Each infantry division had three 105mm howitzer battalions, with 18 guns each.

American forces travel inland from the Normandy beachhead on June 7, 1944—one day after the Allied invasion.

11

A knocked-out Sherman from the fighting in Normandy. During the early days of the ETO, most American tank losses were from German antitank guns rather than enemy tanks.

Meanwhile, back in America, "isolationism" still rang high in the halls of Congress. That ideology, however, was quickly losing steam as Nazi Germany advanced on all fronts. Determined to stem the tide of Nazi aggression, even if by passive measures, Congress passed the Lend-Lease Act in 1941. Under the provisions of Lend-Lease, the U.S. sent several thousand pieces of military equipment to Great Britain and the Soviet Union for their struggles against the Wehrmacht. Still, many Americans hoped that the war in Europe would run its course without their involvement. This quickly changed, however, in the wake of the Japanese attack on Pearl Harbor.

The attack of December 7, 1941, caught most Americans by surprise. To that point, nearly everyone had considered the Japanese military to be an inferior force. Strategic analysts had been convinced that Pearl Harbor, the Navy's principal anchorage in the Pacific, was invulnerable to any Japanese attack. Distance was the supposed ally, while the shallow depth of the harbor did not lend itself to traditional torpedo attacks.

The Imperial Japanese Navy had hoped to crush the U.S. Pacific Fleet in one blow, thus crippling America's ability to wage war. Ironically, they may have succeeded had the U.S.

aircraft carriers not been away from Pearl Harbor on maneuvers. The following day, the U.S. declared war on the Empire of Japan. With the stroke of a pen, America had officially entered World War II. Nazi Germany soon responded by declaring war on the U.S.

Although Japan had made the first strike, the U.S. adopted a "Europe First" strategy. Under these auspices, the U.S. would dedicate most of its military resources to defeating Nazi Germany. The logic behind this decision was that Germany could win the war without Japan, but Japan couldn't win the war without Germany. Thus, the die was cast for an invasion of the European mainland. Getting a toehold on the continent, however, would be a multitiered process: Allied forces would first invade North Africa, defeating Rommel's forces and building a foundation to launch an invasion of Sicily and Italy. By the summer of 1944, the Allies were poised to invade France and make their final push into the heart of the Fatherland. Within a mere three months of the Allied landings in Normandy, the American 4th Armored Division would engage the German 1st Army and 5th Panzer Army in combat at the far edges of eastern France.

Creighton Abrams's tank, "Thunderbolt," takes the lead into a French village.

| American Forces

The European theater showcased the power of American combined arms forces—armor and mechanized infantry. Sherman tanks led the armored spearhead following the Wehrmacht after the Allied landings at Normandy. These Shermans were accompanied into battle by various mechanized assets including the M3-series halftrack and the M8 Greyhound Light Armored Car. For the first two months of the campaign, there were very few tank-on-tank engagements. The battle of Arracourt, however, demonstrated the efficacy of American armor against the best tanks of the Wehrmacht. In engagements large and small, the Sherman proved itself against the likes of the Panzer IV and Panther tanks.

American Equipment

M3/M5 Stuart Light Tank

The M3 Stuart grew out of the U.S. Army's program to improve the M2 Light Tank. Observing actions of the panzer units in Europe, American tank designers realized the M2 couldn't stand toe-to-toe against the latest German armor. Upgrading the M2 with thicker armor, a better suspension, and an improved gun recoil system, the army redesignated it as the "Light Tank, M3." Mass production of the vehicle began in March 1941 and continued until late 1943.

Like its immediate predecessor, the M2A4, the M3 was initially armed with a 37mm main gun and five 30-caliber machine guns. The first machine gun was located coaxially with the main gun, the second on top of the turret, the third mounted on the right bow, with the fourth and fifth machine guns mounted respectively in the left and right hull sponsons. Later, the main gun was replaced with a slightly longer M6 variant, but it retained the 37mm caliber. Also, the sponson machine guns were eventually removed. Despite its designation as a "light tank," the Stuart was surprisingly heavy in its armor. For instance, the upper and lower front hulls had 38mm and 44mm armor plating respectively. Meanwhile, there were 51mm of armor on the gun mantle and 38mm on the turret sides.

Most of the M3 variants built were powered by an air-cooled, seven-cylinder Continental W-670 radial gasoline engine—although nearly 1,500 Stuarts were powered by nine-cylinder Guiberson T-1020 diesel engines. Ironically, both powerplants had originally been developed as aircraft engines. For either engine aboard the M3, it was located at the rear of the tank while the transmission stood in the front of the hull. The engine's crankshaft, however, stood high off the bottom hull, contributing to the tank's high profile.

As wartime demand for radial aero-engines grew, military planners developed a new version of the M3 featuring twin Cadillac V8 automobile engines with twin Hydra-

The M5 Stuart Light Tank. Alongside the M4 Sherman, the M3 and M5 Stuart-series tanks were a mainstay of American armored forces during World War II. In the European theater, American tank battalions typically had one company of light tanks.

Matic transmissions. Labeled the "M5"—since the "M4" designation already belonged to the Sherman tank—this upgraded Stuart was quieter, more spacious, and its automatic transmission simplified crew training. Although several units had complained about the M3's lack of firepower, the M5 nevertheless retained the same 37mm gun. The M5 eventually replaced the M3 in production after 1942, until it was superseded by the M24 Chafee in 1944. In total, more than 8,800 M5 variants were built.

M4 Sherman

Perhaps the most popular tank of World War II, the M4 Sherman was developed as a replacement for the M3 Stuart. Named after the famous American Civil War leader, General William T. Sherman, the M4 was first produced at the Lima Locomotive Works in Lima, Ohio. Throughout its production run, the U.S. Army developed seven successive variants of the M4 Sherman: the M4, M4A1, M4A2, M4A3, M4A4, M4A5, and M4A6. However, these designations did not necessarily represent upgrades or improvements to the base-model M4. Rather, these successive designations represented standardized variations in production (for example, engine configurations and performance metrics). In fact, many of these M4 variants were manufactured concurrently at different production facilities.

Whatever their designation or assigned variant, most Shermans ran on gasoline-powered engines. The M4 and M4A1, for example, ran on a nine-cylinder, air-cooled Wright R975 Whirlwind 9 radial engine, producing up to 400 horsepower. The M4A3 featured a liquid-cooled Ford GAA V8 while the M4A4 used the Chrysler A57 multibank engine. The M4A2 and M4A6, however, ran on diesel engines. The M4A2 carried twin GMC 6–71 in-line engines, while the M4A6 was powered by a nine-cylinder Caterpillar RD-1820.

An M4 Sherman from the 37th Tank Battalion, 4th Armored Division. The tank in this photo fought through Arracourt and is pictured here during the Ardennes offensive. The crew has proudly scribbled "First in Bastogne" on the vehicle's side.

M4 Shermans from the 8th Tank Battalion, 4th Armored Division, pass through Countances, France on July 31, 1944.

Over the course of their production, the M4 variants almost simultaneously underwent several upgrades to their strength and performance—all without changing the tank's basic model number. These upgrades included better suspension, improved ammunition stowage, and stronger armor.

The most iconic tank of the World War II, the M4 Sherman, had a long post-war service life. The U.S. maintained the M4A3E8 "Easy Eight" Sherman in service throughout the Korean War. On the frontlines of Korea, this Sherman fought alongside the M26 Pershing and M46 Patton. The U.S. finally retired the Sherman in 1957. The Israeli Defense Forces used the Sherman throughout the 1960s and 1970s, where it performed admirably in the Six-Day War of 1967. Like many vintage American tanks, the Sherman also served among several Latin American armies through the late 20th century. The last known military to operate the Sherman was the Armed Forces of Paraguay, who retired their last three Shermans in 2018.

Central to any M4 variant, however, was its main gun armament. The earliest production Shermans carried a 75mm medium-velocity gun. Later models—namely the M4A1, M4A2, and M4A3—received a high-velocity 76mm gun mounted to a larger turret. Later into its service life, however, the M4A3 received a 105mm gun and a distinctive rounded mantle. In fact, the Sherman's design team had made provisions for the turret to accommodate multiple calibers of main armament. Aside from the 75mm, 76mm, and 105mm cannons, the Sherman's designers had considered mounting a 3-inch

A pair of M4 Shermans from the 8th Tank Battalion smolder after being hit by German antitank guns, July 31, 1944.

heavy tank gun to the turret of the M4, but quickly discovered that it was too unwieldly for the vehicle's body.

The Sherman entered combat in 1942 during the North Africa campaign. The first frontline Shermans came equipped with the 75mm gun, squaring off against the German Panzer III and Panzer IV tanks. Although the 75mm main gun could penetrate the frontal armor of these early Wehrmacht tanks, the first-generation M4s performed rather poorly against the Panther and Tiger tanks.

M3 Halftrack

Developed from the M3 Scout Car, the M3 Halftrack was the U.S. Army's "jack of all trades." Throughout the war, the U.S. fielded more than 40,000 halftracks of various functions and capabilities. Indeed, halftracks served as personnel carriers, reconnaissance vehicles, self-propelled artillery, antiaircraft artillery, and "tank destroyers." In the military parlance of the day, a tank destroyer was an armored vehicle with enough firepower to destroy enemy tanks, but typically lacked the mobility, maneuverability, or operational flexibility of a tank itself. The halftrack concept, however, was devised to combine the handling of a wheeled vehicle with the cross-country durability of a tracked vehicle.

After a somewhat tumultuous and convoluted design process, the base-model M3 Halftrack was tested by the Army at Aberdeen Proving Grounds in 1941 and was accepted into service soon thereafter. Although the U.S. eventually retired all its halftrack vehicles, the M3 variants had a viable postwar service life in the Israeli Defense Forces—serving in both the Six Day War (1967) and the Yom Kippur conflict (1973).

M3-series Halftrack. During World War II, the Americans and Germans made extensive use of halftracks for their mechanized formations. These vehicles combined the ruggedness of a tracked vehicle with the mobility of a wheeled vehicle. After World War II, however, most militaries abandoned the halftrack concept.

M3 halftrack in action.

M7/M8 Howitzer Motor Carriage (HMC)

In the opening days of World War II, the U.S. Army realized it needed a self-propelled artillery vehicle that could keep pace with its armored formations and pack enough firepower to destroy enemy armor. At first, the army had relegated the role of self-propelled artillery to its halftrack formations, using the modified T-19 Howitzer Motor Carriage (HMC) with its 105mm howitzer. Its performance in the field, however, showed Army planners that any future self-propelled gun would have to be fully tracked. Thus, the army decided to build its next mobile howitzer atop an M3 Lee chassis. The result was the "T32," an open-topped, tracked vehicle mounting a 105mm howitzer. The prototype T32 was accepted for service in February 1942 and renamed "M7."

Mass production began that April, with more than 4,000 units built, many of which were exported to the British Army. As the M4 Sherman tank came online, production of the M7 continued on the basis of the M4's chassis. During the North Africa campaign, the British Eighth Army received 90 M7s, and were the first to use the HMC in combat, delivering fire support to units at the second battle of El Alamein. Both American and British forces used the M7 throughout the European theater and, by 1943, the M7 had become the backbone for the armored division's artillery forces. The M7 continued in service well into the Korean War, but was eventually supplanted by the M37 HMC, built atop the chassis of an M24 light tank.

Almost simultaneously with the M7, the U.S. developed the remarkably similar M8. Built atop an M5 Stuart chassis, the M8 was initially designated the "T47," which carried a 75mm howitzer. Aside from its new armament, and an open-topped turret, the M8 was virtually identical to the M5 Stuart. Like its M5 forebearer, the M8 HMC also had a crew of four: the vehicle commander, gunner, driver, and loader.

M7 Howitzer Motor Carriages (HMC). Mounted atop an M3 chassis, the M7 was a self-propelled artillery mount that could keep pace with the M4 Sherman on the battlefield. The U.S. Army made extensive use of the M7-series HMC well into the Korean War.

An M7 HMC prepares for a fire mission.

For a self-propelled howitzer, the M8 was fast and nimble. But, much like the M5, it had relatively thin armor. The lower hull, for instance, featured armor that ranged from only 1 to 1.125 inches (25mm to 28.6mm) in thickness. The M8's most powerful asset, however, was its 75mm M2 (and later, M3) howitzer. The M8 carried 46 rounds of 75mm ammunition, the most common of which were the M48 high-explosive shells and the M89 white phosphorus ("Willie Pete") shells. The white phosphorus rounds were among the deadliest conventional munitions on the battlefield. Instead of being a pure incendiary round, white phosphorus was a chemical coating designed to, literally, burn the flesh from an enemy's bones. As a secondary armament, the M8 was equipped with a Browning M2HB .50-caliber machine gun for local defense or antiaircraft missions.

Like its M7 counterpart, the M8 was a mainstay of the heavy artillery battalions during World War II. In 1944, however, production of the M8 was phased out in favor of the newer M4-based HMCs with heavier firepower. Throughout its service life, more than 1,770 M8 HMCs were built.

M8 Greyhound Light Armored Car

The M8 Light Armored Car was a 6×6 armored car developed by the Ford Motor Company, used by both American and British forces. Developed primarily for reconnaissance, the M8 had somewhat of a tumultuous design process. In fact, the M8 Greyhound began life as a prototype tank destroyer. In July 1941, the Ordnance Department announced the development of a wheeled tank destroyer to replace the tracked gun motor carriages. The anticipated high-speed platform was essentially a six-wheeled, three-quarter-ton truck with a 37mm gun. The truck would be lightly armored, with enough protection to stop the normal variety of Axis small arms—including 7.62 and 12.7mm ammunition. Answering the call for designs, Studebaker, Ford, and Chrysler submitted prototypes, all of which were similar in design and appearance.

The War Department accepted Ford's design in April 1942, but it was clear that the 37mm gun couldn't fulfill its role of destroying enemy tanks. Thus, the newly designated "M8" became a reconnaissance vehicle, wherein its main gun would fulfill a primarily defensive role. Although the final 6×6 prototype was visually impressive, the British Tank Mission initially declined to accept the M8 through Lend-Lease, although the British Army later accepted some 496 units before the end of the war. It was in British service that the M8 earned its nickname, the "Greyhound," in keeping with other American armored cars serving in the British Army, including the T17 Deerhound and the T17E1 Staghound.

American serial production began in March 1943. The M8 was powered by a Hercules Model JXD six-cylinder engine, which gave it a top speed of 55mph (88km/h) on-road, and 30mph (48km/h) off-road. For an armored combat vehicle, its mileage was better than most, with an average fuel consumption of 7.5 miles per gallon and road endurance of 200–400 miles (320–640 kilometers). The Hercules JXD also ran quieter than other engines, which added to the M8's stealthy reconnaissance capabilities. Indeed, the M8 Greyhounds were known as "Patton's ghosts" because they were difficult to detect.

Carrying a crew of four—commander (who doubled as the loader), gunner, driver, and radio operator—the M8's hull armor was only 0.5 inches to 0.75 inches thick at its strongest points. The floor was even less armored, carrying only 0.25 inches of protection, thereby increasing its susceptibility to landmines. The turret, however, was comparatively better protected, featuring 0.75 inches of armor encasing.

M8 Greyhound Light Armored Car. A 6×6 reconnaissance vehicle designed by the Ford Motor Company, the M8 was among the fastest vehicles in the Allied inventory. It carried a 37mm main gun and was known for its stealth. The M8s within the Third U.S. Army were known as "Patton's Ghosts" due to their quiet-running engines.

German soldiers wrangle two captured M8 Greyhounds abandoned by their Allied crews. (Top: Bundesarchiv, Bild 101I-301-1955-14/ Kurth; above: Bundesarchiv, Bild 101I-301-1970-20)

The M8's primary armament was its 37mm M6 main gun, for which the vehicle carried 80 rounds—16 in the turret and 64 in the sponson ammunition rack. The 80-round capacity, however, could only be achieved if the vehicle were equipped with one radio. Vehicles with two radios could only carry 16 main gun rounds. Some units, however, solved this problem by modifying the ammunition rack to hold an additional 36 rounds underneath the radios. The secondary armaments included a coaxially mounted 7.62mm machine gun and a .50-caliber Browning M2HB machine gun, which could be used for both ground and air defense purposes. For these secondary machine guns, the vehicle carried 1,500 rounds of 7.62mm ammunition and 400 rounds of .50-caliber bullets. Each vehicle also carried 16 hand grenades (smoke and incendiary) in addition to six antitank mines.

Throughout its time in American service, the M8 was used as a reconnaissance asset, given to cavalry troops and squadrons with the American divisions. Acting as the "eyes and ears" for the division commander on the battlefield, these M8 units traveled in front (and alongside the flanks) of a main body's advance, surveilling and reporting enemy activity. Their mission relied on speed and agility, rather than pure firepower. If the cavalry unit

The M8 Greyhound Armored Car was a proverbial "mixed bag." Although the vehicle crews admired its speed and handling on-road, they were less enthusiastic about its off-road performance. Ironically, American cavalry scouts preferred using the Willys Jeep for mounted reconnaissance. The M8 was, however, among the quietest-running vehicles in the Allied inventory, which aided its role as a reconnaissance vehicle.

made contact with enemy forces, they would maintain it long enough to assess the enemy's size and strength before handing off the battle to the main units.

The M8 excelled in its reconnaissance role, but crews often criticized it for its poor suspension and off-road handling. With a combat weight of 17,400 pounds (7,900 kilograms), it was somewhat heavy for a wheeled reconnaissance vehicle, and it performed better when traveling on highways and improved surfaces. In fact, most units preferred using the garden-variety Jeep as a reconnaissance vehicle in wooded terrain.

Production of the M8 continued until June 1945. A total of 8,523 M8 Greyhounds were built before production ended in 1945. Unlike many of its World War II stablemates, however, the M8 Greyhound had a long postwar service life. Several M8s remained in service with the postwar constabulary during the occupation of Europe, and later served as military police vehicles during the Korean War. At nearly the same time, many M8s were donated to the French Army, where they served in the First Indochina War and the Algerian Revolution. Consequently, many of the latter-day French M8s were passed on to the Army of the Republic of Vietnam (ARVN), where they saw action during the early days of the Vietnam War. During the latter part of the 20th century, many ex-American M8s found their way into the armies of Latin America. As of 2021, the M8 Greyhound continues in service with the Colombian, Paraguayan, and Peruvian armies.

Crews from the 25th Cavalry Squadron pose in front of an M8 Armored Car. The 25th Cavalry were the proverbial "eyes and ears" for the 4th Armored Division, screening, conducting reconnaissance, and providing an early warning system for the main-body units of the division.

In Profile:
General George S. Patton

General George S. Patton, commander of the Third U.S. Army, to which the 4th Armored Division belonged.

A 1909 West Point graduate, Patton was one of the inaugural commanders in the U.S. Tank Corps during World War I, leading the hastily assembled and trained American tank crews into combat over the trenches of Western Europe. During the interwar years, he fought steadily to maintain some semblance of an armored force within the U.S. defense structure. By the outset of World War II, he was on the frontlines fighting the Nazis in North Africa and in Europe. His command of the U.S. Third Army became one of the focal points in the drive to the Fatherland. Known for his flamboyant personality and "piss-and-vinegar" style of leadership, Patton was both admired and detested by many who knew him. After surviving two world wars, however, Patton's life was ironically cut short due to complications following an automobile accident in December 1945.

M18 Hellcat Gun Motor Carriage (GMC)

The M18 Hellcat GMC was a fully tracked "tank destroyer" with an impressive service record. In fact, throughout the war, the M18 achieved a higher kill–loss ratio than any other armored vehicle fielded by American forces. Throughout its service history, it was also the fastest armored vehicle in America's inventory.

In 1941, Lieutenant Colonel Andrew D. Bruce, the inaugural commander of the U.S. Army's Tank Destroyer Force, envisioned his units being equipped with something faster than a tank, but with a stronger gun, and lighter armor for maximum speed. Essentially, he wanted a "cruiser rather than a battleship." He was no fan of the Sherman-based tank destroyers, particularly the M10 and M36, as he deemed them too slow and unwieldy for his needs. He was likewise unfond of the M3 Halftrack tank destroyers.

In December 1941, after several abortive experiments that tested various armaments and armor configurations, the Ordnance Department issued a design requirement for a fast tank destroyer that used a Christie suspension, a Wright-Continental R-975 radial engine, and a 37mm gun. The winning design came from Harley Earl in the Buick Division of General Motors. Using the best automotive technology of the day, Buick's engineers designed a prototype M18 with a torsion bar suspension to provide a steady ride. The nine-cylinder Wright-Continental R-975 engine generated nearly 400 horsepower and was paired to a 900T Torqmatic automatic transmission. This configuration gave the Hellcat a top traveling speed of 55mph (88.5km/h), all within a 20-ton tare weight.

During the developmental and testing stage, General Motors evaluated the Hellcat in a similar manner to how they tested their passenger vehicles. Indeed, at GM's Milford

M18 Hellcat Tank Destroyer. The M18 was a relative latecomer to the war but achieved an impressive kill record during its brief service. By definition, a "tank destroyer" is a vehicle that has enough punch to stop a tank, but typically has less mobility and/or armored protection than a tank itself.

An M18 Hellcat provides overwatch at an intersection in Lunéville, September 1944. The M18 was as much an infantry support weapon as it was an antitank platform.

Proving Ground, the M18 Hellcat was tested on a flat, paved road course followed by a rough road course. The military-specific portion of the test included a fording obstacle (six feet of water), small vertical obstacles, and a test of the M18's ability to ram various structures.

The army was impressed by the prototype but requested replacing the 37mm with a heavier gun. The 37mm armament, they said, just didn't pack enough of an "armored punch" to destroy the newest iteration of Panzer and Tiger tanks. Eventually, the Hellcat upgraded its armament to a 76mm main gun and began full production in July 1943.

The first-model Hellcats were delivered on a test-run basis to the 704th Tank Destroyer Battalion. Originally trained on the M3 Halftracks, the 704th took a strong liking to the Hellcat. Despite noting several areas for improvement, the battalion remarked the vehicle had been "superlative" in its performance. These field tests also proved that teamwork, tight communication, and low-level initiative were essential to the tank destroyer's success. This in turn would precipitate a new, flexible command structure that allowed vehicle crews and sections to be more adaptive and responsive to changes on the battlefield. After General Motors and the Ordnance Department incorporated the 704th's suggestions into the final product, the battalion received the first production-run Hellcats in 1944.

Despite its impressive kill record, the M18 was a relative latecomer to the war, arriving at the battlefront in 1944. The prototype variants first saw action at the Anzio beachhead; the first production-run Hellcats saw action in France and Germany following the Normandy invasion. A smaller number of Hellcats served in the Pacific theater, supporting the American drive into the Philippines and Okinawa. After the war, the M18 Hellcat saw limited service in Korea and was exported to various Allied states including Yugoslavia, Greece, Taiwan, and Venezuela. At this writing, Venezuela is the only country that still maintains a fleet of Hellcats.

U.S. 4th Armored Division

At the outset of World War II, the U.S. Army lagged behind the Wehrmacht in terms of its armored capabilities. Since the end of World War I, American tanks had been relegated to the infantry as little more than "support weapons." Indeed, as late as 1938, the *horse cavalry* was still the U.S. Army's most mobile and rapid strike force. Taking note of the blitzkrieg in Europe, however, the War Department authorized development of the M1 Light Tank and subsequently created the Armored Force on July 15, 1940. Under the leadership of General Adna Chaffee, separate brigades at Fort Knox and Fort Benning formed the backbone of the inaugural armored divisions. From these humble beginnings, Armored Force grew to 16 armored divisions by the end of World War II. Starting with less than 1,000 World War I–era tanks in 1940, the U.S. had produced nearly 90,000 tanks by 1945.

Among the first of these numbered divisions was the 4th Armored Division. Activated on April 15, 1941, at Pine Camp, New York (present-day Fort Drum), the division had an initial cadre of 3,800 men. Growing steadily in its size and personnel, the unit was constituted as a full-strength armored division by the summer of 1942. Throughout the war, it was one of the few American divisions not to adopt an official nickname. Whereas other armored divisions adopted colorful nicknames like "Old Ironsides" and "Hell on Wheels," the 4th Armored Division was simply known as "Name Enough," owing to its commander's remark: "Fourth Armored Division is name enough. They shall be known by their deeds alone." Invariably, they were also known as "Patton's Best," for their distinguished combat record in service to the Third U.S. Army.

General Manton Eddy (left), the commander of the U.S. XX Corps, confers with General John Wood, commander of the 4th Armored Division. Wood led the division in combat throughout its time in the ETO.

The 4th Armored Division undergoes maneuver training in England before landing on Utah Beach, 1944.

After reaching full strength, the division departed Pine Camp for Camp Forrest, Tennessee, partaking in maneuvers throughout the Cumberland Mountains in September/October 1942. More maneuvers followed throughout 1942 and 1943, including stints at the Camp Ibis Desert Training Center and finally at Camp Myles Standish for extensive winter training. On December 29, 1943, the 4th Armored Division departed Boston for the Allied staging areas in England. For the next seven months, the division prepared for the invasion of Normandy.

For operations in the European Theater of Operations (ETO), the 4th Armored Division was assigned to Patton's Third Army. The Third Army typically had three to four armored divisions on hand, along with a few separate tank battalions and tank destroyer battalions. Of the American armored divisions assigned to the Third Army, the 4th Armored Division, and the 2d French Armored Division were the most reliable. The 7th Armored Division was Patton's proverbial "problem child," owing to its lackluster command teams. The 6th Armored Division, meanwhile, was tried and true, but it arrived too late to have any impact on the battle of Arracourt.

Unlike the infantry divisions, which were organized into brigades, the U.S. armored divisions were organized into "combat commands": Combat Command A, Combat Command B, and Combat Command R (Reserve). These combat commands had no fixed subordinate units—the subordinate battalions could float amongst the different commands depending on the operational needs of a given day. Each combat command typically had at least one tank battalion, an armored infantry battalion, and a field artillery battalion.

All of the American armored divisions under Patton's command were so-called "light" divisions. These organizations were structured according to the 1943 Table of Organization & Equipment (TO&E). Under this structural layout, the American "light" divisions contained three tank battalions, three artillery battalions, and three infantry battalions. As a whole, the armored divisions were structured differently from infantry divisions. Instead of the customary "brigades," the armored divisions were organized

The 4th Armored Division on parade in England prior to its departure, July 1944.

into "combat commands." Each armored division had three combat commands that were comparable in size to an infantry brigade—Combat Command A (CCA), Combat Command B (CCB), and Combat Command Reserve (CCR). The latter of the three, CCR, was a "revolving door" of sorts, where battle-weary battalions could rest and refit before getting back into the fight. Unlike the infantry brigades, combat commands did not have a fixed organizational structure. Indeed, many of the subordinate battalions floated between CCA and CCB on any given day, depending on the mission. For example, CCA might have two armored infantry battalions and a tank battalion for one day's mission; then have two tank battalions and an artillery battalion for the following day's mission.

In Profile:
American Armor

Opposite The M3-series halftrack sought to combine the cross-country mobility of a tracked vehicle with the handling of a wheeled vehicle. Found mostly in armored units, the M3 halftrack was adapted to a variety of battlefield functions, most notably as an armored personnel carrier and a tank destroyer. Most Western militaries discontinued the use of half-tracks after World War II.

Conceived as an armored car and reconnaissance vehicle, the 6x6 Greyhound was a mainstay of mechanized cavalry units during World War II. It had a higher road speed than other armored vehicles, and its engine was immensely quiet, thereby giving the vehicle a tactical edge in the game of reconnaissance. In fact, throughout Patton's Third Army, the M8s were known as "Patton's Ghosts" due to the silent running of their engines.

Opposite As a tank destroyer, the M18 lacked the armored protection of most Allied tanks, but its accomplishments were no less impressive. Featuring a 76mm main gun, the Hellcat had the highest speed of any American tracked vehicle. Although it was a relative latecomer to the war (arriving in 1944), it achieved the highest kill-loss ratio of any American tank or tank destroyer in World War II. The M18 remained in service through the Korean War, and remains in limited service with the Venezuelan Army today.

For duty in Europe, the 4th Armored Division's organic units were as follows:

- 8th Tank Battalion
- 35th Tank Battalion
- 37th Tank Battalion
- 10th Armored Infantry Battalion
- 51st Armored Infantry Battalion
- 53d Armored Infantry Battalion
- 25th Cavalry Reconnaissance Squadron (Mechanized)
- 24th Armored Engineer Battalion
- 144th Armored Signal Company
- 22d Armored Field Artillery Battalion
- 66th Armored Field Artillery Battalion
- 94th Armored Field Artillery Battalion
- 126th Ordnance Maintenance Battalion
- 4th Armored Medical Battalion

The tank battalions had six companies each: a headquarters company, a service company, three companies of M4 medium tanks (A, B, and C), and a company of M5 light tanks (D Company). The headquarters section was equipped with Jeeps and halftracks plus two medium tanks: one for the battalion commander and one for his second-in-command.

The armored infantry battalions, meanwhile, relied on the M2 and M3 troop-carrier halftracks. In practice, the armored infantry battalions used the halftrack as little more than a "battlefield taxi," carrying troops into battle where they would fight dismounted. For pursuit operations, however, the infantrymen would remount the halftracks for greater speed and mobility. Each of the line companies in the armored infantry battalion had a headquarters section, along with three rifle platoons and an antitank platoon. The headquarters section had two M3A1 halftracks, two 2.5-ton trucks, and two Jeeps. Each rifle platoon had five M3A1 halftracks—three for each rifle squad, one for the mortar squad, and one for the machine-gun squad. The antitank platoon, curiously, did not feature the GMC halftrack, but instead carried three 57mm antitank guns, each of which was towed by a standard M3A1 halftrack.

In the infantry divisions, artillery battalions fell under jurisdiction of the Division Artillery (DIVARTY). For units like the 4th Armored Division, however, artillery battalions were attached ad hoc to whichever combat command needed them. In the American armored divisions, artillery units were fully mechanized whereas most of the German Army was still using towed artillery. The standard mount used by the 4th Armored Division's batteries was the M7 HMC. Although the M7 allowed its artillerymen to keep pace with the M4 Sherman and M5 Stuart, it lacked the firepower of the heavier 155mm howitzer found in the infantry divisions. Thus, it was not uncommon to see a 155mm howitzer battalion attached to an armored division for operations that required heavy fire support. The 4th Armored Division thus had the 191st Field Artillery Battalion providing its 155mm indirect fire for the battle at Arracourt.

Lieutenant Colonel Creighton Abrams, commander of the 37th Tank Battalion, proudly stands by his tank, which he nicknamed "Thunderbolt." Abrams developed the habit of nicknaming his vehicles "Thunderbolt," and the moniker soon became synonymous with Abrams himself. The 37th Tank Battalion was one of the most decorated units with the 4th Armored Division. Abrams himself would later command American forces in Vietnam and serve as Chief of Staff of the Army.

Aside from its artillery support, the 4th Armored Division had also had the 704th Tank Destroyer Battalion attached to its ranks. These tank destroyer battalions were created as a direct response to the brutal efficiency of Germany's panzer divisions in the early days of World War II. After wading through the after-action reports and raw footage of the blitzkrieg campaign, U.S. Army planners wanted a tank destroyer force to stem the tide of any hordes of panzer attacks.

Major General John S. Wood (center), commander of the 4th Armored Division, confers with Generals Omar Bradley (left) and George Patton (right) during a pause in offensive operations, 1944.

American soldiers inspect the remains of a knocked-out Panther in Normandy, June 1944.

Another German tank lies in ruin following Operation *Cobra* on July 25, 1944. The successful completion of *Cobra* put American forces closer to the borders of the Reich.

The largest panzer operation prior to Lorraine was Operation *Lüttich*, the purpose of which was to halt the forward elements of the Third Army at Avranches. The operation failed and the Third Army rolled right along. Pictured here are two Panther tanks and an Sd.Kfz. halftrack, casualties of the firefight.

More evidence of American handiwork following Operation *Lüttich*.

Although the 4th Armored Division was one of the few American armored divisions not to adopt an "official" nickname during the war, the division later adopted the nickname "Breakthrough" in 1954. That nickname, however, was eventually discontinued. After the war, parts of the division were assigned to the First Constabulary Brigade during the postwar reconstruction of Germany. The entire division later served along the Iron Curtain as part of the ongoing defense of West Germany. The division was deactivated for good, however, in 1971.

By 1943, however, it became clear that the blitzkrieg-style panzer formations were a thing of the past. Thus, the tank destroyer battalions were attached to divisions as an additional antitank force. The 704th, like other tank destroyer battalions, had three companies equipped with 12 M18 Hellcats each. Other units within the Third Army, however, were still using the M10-series GMC.

The 25th Cavalry Reconnaissance Squadron provided the "eyes and ears" for the division's main body units. Every armored division had a similar squadron, consisting of four reconnaissance troops. Each troop was equipped with the M8 Greyhound light armored car and four M3 halftracks. These cavalry assets were expected to provide flank security, forward surveillance, and mobile reconnaissance—all of which were intended to inform the main body units of enemy activity, size, and disposition. If attacked, these recon elements were not expected to decisively engage the enemy but return fire long enough to allow for a tactical egress and "hand off" the battle to the follow-on main body forces.

The 4th Armored Division landed at Utah Beach on July 11, 1944 and saw its first combat action six days later. The following week, the division took part in Operation *Cobra*, securing the area around Coutances as part of the VIII Corps' exploitation force. Within a mere two months, the men of "Patton's Best" would be on a collision course with the 5th Panzer Army at Arracourt.

An M4 Sherman from the 8th Tank Battalion passes through Avranches during the breakout from Normandy, August 1944.

German Forces

By the time of the Allied invasion, the Wehrmacht was stretched beyond its ability to properly defend the Reich. Still, the Germans made good use of what limited resources they had. Leading the defense of Occupied France and the German borderlands were the Panzer IV and Panther tanks, both of which had proved formidable in earlier campaigns.

The Germans' defensive postures were supplemented by a number of French-built forts along the countryside, excellent redoubts on the Allied avenues of advance. As the Americans approached Arracourt, however, it became clear that the German tanks had been optimized for engagements at standoff distances. They fared rather poorly in close-quarter combat against the M4 Sherman and M18 Tank Destroyers

German Equipment

Panzer IV

The Panzerkampfwagen IV (Pz.Kpfw IV), or simply Panzer IV, was the latest iteration of German tanks that bore the name "Panzer." The term *panzer* itself is the German word for "tank," and the earlier-model Panzers I through III bore different designs and capabilities than the Panzer IV. By design, the Panzer IV was a "medium tank," which represented a compromise between the rapid mobility of "light tanks" and the firepower of "heavy

Panzer IV tank. One of the most ubiquitous German tanks of the war, the Panzer IV was developed as a counterbalance to the Soviet T-34. The tank fought on all major German fronts during World War II. Although respected by Axis and Allies alike, its reliability and overall construction was comparable to the M4 Sherman. (Bundesarchiv, Bild 101I-297-1725-11 / Kurth / CC-BY-SA 3.0)

A heavily camouflaged Panzer IV tank prepares for action on the outskirts of Normandy. As the Allies broke through Caen and Carentan, the Wehrmacht began sending in more of its panzers to stem the tide of the Allied advance. (Bundesarchiv, Bild 101I-301-1955-32 / Kurth / CC-BY-SA 3.0)

tanks." Second only to the Sturmgeschütz III, the Panzer IV was the most-produced German armored vehicle of World War II, with some 8,500 units built. Its chassis also became the basis for many other fighting vehicles, including the Sturmgeschütz IV and the Jagdpanzer IV.

Developed in the late 1930s, the Panzer IV served in *every* German theater from North Africa to the Eastern Front. Initially, the Panzer IV was designed as an infantry support vehicle, while the Panzer III was intended to fight enemy tanks. This notion changed, however, when the German panzer armies met the Soviet T-34 in battle. Realizing that the Panzer IV had more potential for tank-on-tank warfare (given its larger turret ring) the Panzer III was relegated to infantry support, while the Panzer IV took on the mantle of armored warfare.

It was also the only German tank to remain in continuous production throughout World War II, receiving numerous upgrades and design modifications. There were several variants of the Panzer IV, each lettered "A" through "J"—many of which received upgrades to their armament. Variant H (*Ausführung* H), for example, sported the KwK 40 main gun. The KwK was among the deadliest field guns in the Wehrmacht, with a muzzle velocity of 2,500 feet per second (750 meters per second) and a maximum range of nearly 8,000 meters (5 miles). Despite its ubiquity, however, the Panzer IV was partially succeeded by the Panther tank—with the latter being touted as a true contender against the T-34. Still, the Panzer IV continued to play a significant role in the German panzer armies until the end of the war.

Aside from being the most mass-produced tank of the Wehrmacht, it was also the most widely exported. Nearly 300 units were sold to Axis partners including Finland, Bulgaria, Spain, and Romania. After the war, Syria acquired a number of Panzer IVs, many of which saw combat during the Six-Day War in 1967.

Panther Tank

Developed in 1938 as an eventual replacement for the Panzer III and Panzer IV, the Panther tank did not deploy until 1943, where it first served on the Eastern Front. The Panther was initially designated as "Panzerkampfwagen V Panther," until Hitler ordered the Roman numeral "V" dropped from its listing. Developed as a counter to the Soviet T-34, the Panther served alongside its stablemates, the Panzer IV and the Tiger I, until the end of the war.

Although renowned for its firepower and protection, it was mechanically less reliable than many of its contemporaries. The Panther was, in many ways, a victim of its own rushed production. To meet Hitler's production demands, the Panther went to the assembly line before many of its mechanical and design issues had been resolved. Many of these design flaws were corrected over time, but others, such as the weak drivetrain units, were never fully corrected.

Although classified as a "medium tank," the Panther weighed in at nearly 45 metric tons, thereby making it more comparable to the heavy tanks of its day, including the American M26 Pershing and the Soviet IS-2. The vehicle carried a crew of five: the commander, gunner,

Widely considered to be one of the best tanks of World War II, the Panther had excellent armor and firepower. Although feared by Allied tank crews, the Panther's Achilles heel was its weak side armor, which made it vulnerable to flanking shots. (Bundesarchiv, Bild 101I-711-0427-04 / Theodor Scheerer / CC-BY-SA 3.0)

A pair of knocked-out Panther tanks lie in similar states of disrepair along the Vire River after the initial clashes of July 11, 1944.

loader, driver, and radio operator. Powered by a Maybach V12 engine similar to that found on the Tiger I, the Panther operated on a unique suspension system. Perhaps one of its most distinctive features was the double-interleaving road wheels, suspended on a dual torsion bar suspension. This torsion bar system, designed by Ernst Lehr, allowed the Panther to maintain high speeds of travel over rough and undulating terrain. Despite its girth, the tank had a very high power-to-weight ratio, thereby making it a highly mobile and fast armored platform.

The Panther itself was a bit of a compromise. It had virtually the same powerplant as the Tiger I, but its KwK 42 main gun had a higher muzzle velocity and better armor-piercing capabilities. The Panther was also lighter and faster, thereby making it a better cross-country tank than the vaunted Tiger I. The tradeoff, however, was that the Panther had thinner side armor. This rendered the tank vulnerable to flanking fire. Still, the Panther proved to be a deadly combatant in open terrain and from standoff distances. It was also cheaper to produce than the Tiger, and only slightly more expensive than the earlier-generation panzers. Although deadly in combat, many tank crewmen complained that the Panther was "over-engineered," and that its maintenance was more costly and time-consuming than other tanks in the Wehrmacht.

The Panther first saw combat during the battle of Kursk in 1943. It performed adequately in combat, but its numerous unresolved technical problems led to high losses on the battlefield. The Wehrmacht, however, rectified many of these design flaws by early 1944, whereafter the tank performed more admirably in successive battles. Unlike other German tanks, the Panther's production variants did not follow the alphabetical order designation. The inaugural edition of the Panther was the "D" variant, soon followed by variants "A" and "G."

The Panzer IV tanks were among the most ubiquitous of the Germany Army. However, their reliability and performance were more on par with the M4 Sherman than most historians realize. The Panther, however, was formidable foe on the battlefield, but even the Panther had its drawbacks. It had a powerful main gun and strong frontal armor, but its side armor was lacking. American tank crews took full advantage of the weak points and often engaged the Panther with flanking shots.

A Panther tank abandoned by its crew after the fighting at Mairy.

The Panther variants continued in service until the end of the war. During the latter stages of the Eastern Front campaign, the Red Army captured several Panthers and put them into Soviet service after repainting them with the red star emblem. After the war, some surviving Panthers remained in limited service with the Romanian and Bulgarian armies until 1950.

With its characteristic interlaced road wheels, this battered Panther prepares for another day of combat. By the time the 4th Armored Division reached Arracourt, the number of operational Panthers and Panzer IVs was falling at an alarming rate. (Bundesarchiv, Bild 101I-301-1958-22 / Genzler)

Sturmgeschütz III

With more than 10,000 units produced, the Sturmgeschütz III (StuG III) was the most-produced German armored vehicle of the war. By definition, the StuG III was an "assault gun." The assault gun was neither a "tank" nor a "tank destroyer," but rather a self-propelled artillery piece that provided direct-fire support to infantry. During World War II, however, assault guns could be used as either direct or indirect fire artillery. And although they had comparable firepower to a tank, they often had lower muzzle velocities, which made them well suited for knocking out buildings, bunkers, and other fortified positions. They were never intended to fight and maneuver as tank substitutes, nor were they intended to operate as tank destroyers. Nevertheless, given the battlefield dynamics of the war, many assault guns were forced to engage enemy armor while defending infantry. These lessons eventually prompted the postwar armies to abandon the assault gun in favor of more versatile armored vehicles such as the main battle tank.

On June 15, 1936, Daimler-Benz AG received an order from the Wehrmacht to develop an infantry support vehicle that could accommodate a high-caliber mounted artillery gun. Based on the German Army's experience in World War I, the Nazi high command wanted to give the infantry a more lethal means to attack enemy fortifications. The current arsenal of artillery was deemed too heavy and not mobile enough to keep pace with the advancing infantry. Thus, to destroy enemy bunkers, pillboxes, and other fortifications, German troops would need a self-propelled, direct-fire gun with cross-country mobility.

At more than 10,000 units built, the StuG III was the most-produced armored vehicle in the Wehrmacht. As an "assault gun," the StuG III was primarily an infantry support weapon, designed to knock down enemy fortifications and the like.

A knocked-out StuG III, presumably from the 111th Panzer Brigade, near Lunéville.
September 18, 1944.

Another knocked-out StuG III near Lunéville.

To create its new assault gun, Daimler-Benz recycled the chassis and drivetrain of the Panzer III, modified with a casemate superstructure and sporting a fixed 7.5cm main gun. The main gun, however, had a limited traversing range of about 25°. Thus, the StuG III would not have the same responsiveness, or even the same situational awareness, as a tank. Early model StuG IIIs were fitted with a low-velocity StuK 37 L/24 gun, similar to the first-generation Panzer IVs. The attendant low-velocity shells were thinly built and carried a high-explosive charge—ideal ammunition to destroy soft-skinned targets and enemy fortifications.

Both Axis and Allies made extensive use of halftrack vehicles. For the Allies, it was the M3 halftrack; for the Axis, it was the Sd.Kfz. 251 series. Both sides used the halftracks for their mechanized infantry forces, claiming that it combined the best aspects of wheeled and track vehicles. Halftracks, however, largely fell out of favor by the end of the World War II, and most militaries had discontinued their usage by the early 1960s.

When the StuG III entered service in 1940, it was not immediately clear which branch of the German Army would assume control of the weapon. It was, technically, a "self-propelled artillery gun," but it was not an indirect-fire weapon. It was a tracked vehicle, but neither the panzer corps nor the motorized infantry had the resources to accommodate it. The StuG III was thus given to the artillery corps. Still, these assault gun units were largely autonomous and were attached to infantry formations as needed.

The StuG III served until the end of World War II, but its postwar service life was cut short as the assault gun concept was abandoned by most militaries around the world. Like the Panzer IV, however, a handful of StuG IIIs were donated to Syria, many of which saw action during the Six-Day War.

Sd.Kfz. 251 Halftrack

The Axis version of the M3 halftrack was the Sonderkraftfahrzeug, commonly abbreviated as "Sd.Kfz." Throughout the war, there were several iterations of the Sd.Kfz. The model 251 was primarily an armored personnel carrier, designed to transport panzergrenadiers into battle. Many, however, were adapted with antitank guns similar to what the Allies had done with the M3 GMC. Several thousand variants of the Sd.Kfz. were built, many of which saw action during the Western European campaigns.

There were four main variants of the Sd.Kfz. 251 (*Ausführung* A through D). These lettered variants, in turn, served as the basis for at least 22 sub-variants, each with a different function and slightly different modifications. Delivered to the Wehrmacht in 1939, the Sd.Kfz. 251 featured a machine gun as its primary armament (either an MG 34 or MG 42), although some variants were later equipped with high-caliber cannons such as the PaK 36 and the KwK 37 L/24.

Although an "armored" vehicle, its armored protection was such that it could only defend the crew from small-arms fire and perhaps the lowest-caliber armor-piercing rounds. The open-top crew compartment, however, allowed for greater situational awareness and faster egress by the onboard panzergrenadiers. The tradeoff, however, was that the open-top

Sd.Kfz. 251. Much like the Allies' M3 Halftrack, the Sd.Kfz. 251 was the German Army's mechanized "jack of all trades." It was primarily an armored personnel carrier but was adapted to several other uses including a field gun and mortar carrier.

left the backseat riders exposed to enemy aircraft, artillery, and mortar fire. Like many of its tracked counterparts, the Sd.Kfz. 251 also had the Schachtellaufwerk system of overlapping road wheels. This provided better traction but at the cost of more time spent in maintenance and repair.

Tank destroyers and assault guns were remarkably similar in their size and scope. Both lacked the characteristics of a modern tank, but nonetheless provided a heavy direct-fire capability to support the infantry. Assault guns were designed to take on enemy fortifications while tank destroyers, as the name implies, hunted enemy tanks. Based on situational exigencies, however, assault guns and tank destroyers often acted as impromptu tanks. Their success in these roles, however, was as varied as the circumstances themselves.

Halftracks, like their assault gun counterparts, were largely abandoned after World War II. In fact, by the mid-1960s, most NATO armies had retired their halftrack fleets. The Czech Army, however, continued to use an updated version of the Sd.Kfz. 251 until 1995. This Czech version, dubbed the "OT-810," featured a fully enclosed troop compartment and was touted as the next-generation troop carrier for the nuclear battlefield. Understandably, however, Czech soldiers despised the vehicle for its Wehrmacht roots, often calling it "Hitler's Revenge." The few surviving OT-810s are used for display and demonstration purposes.

Jagdpanzer IV

The Jagdpanzer IV (literally "hunting tank") was a turretless tank destroyer based on the Panzer IV chassis. It was developed as a replacement for the StuG III, but Heinz Guderian (who had commanded the 2d Panzer Army on the Eastern Front), saw the Jagdpanzer as needless. He argued that the StuG III could adequately handle the role of a tank destroyer, and that developing the Jagdpanzer would divert resources away from the Panzer IV's production. In the end, however, Guderian lost that argument, and the Jagdpanzer went forward as a dedicated tank destroyer.

Based on their experiences at Stalingrad in September 1942, the Wehrmacht issued a call for a new standard heavy assault gun. According to the specifications, the new self-propelled mount needed 100mm of frontal armor, 40–50mm of side armor, with wider tracks than the existing StuG III and the lowest possible silhouette. This new Panzerjäger ("tank hunter") design would be fitted with the same high-caliber main gun found on the Panther. Installing this heavy gun, however, meant that the Jagdpanzer IV would be top-heavy, considering the weight of the armament combined with the frontal armor. This top-heavy design impacted the Jagdpanzer's mobility and made the vehicle more difficult to operate in rough terrain. By the end of the war, the Jagdpanzer crews had gone to nicknaming the vehicle "Guderian's duck."

The Jagdpanzer IV was technically a "tank destroyer" but also served as an "assault gun." It performed well in its tank-destroying duties but was often called upon as an impromptu tank itself. Given its virtually non-existent traversing capabilities, it did not always do well in the latter role.

A knocked-out M4 Sherman and Jagdpanzer IV near Dieulouard after the 4th Armored Division and 80th Infantry Division overran the German panzergrenadiers.

Series production of the Jagdpanzer IV began in January 1944, with the first variants arriving on the frontlines that spring. As a frontline tank destroyer, the Jagdpanzer IV was assigned to the antitank sections of the panzer and SS panzer divisions. It served admirably in both the Eastern Front and Normandy campaigns, owing much of its success to its low profile, heavy armor, and powerful main gun. Understandably, though, it fared poorly when used as a tank substitute, or even as a direct-fire support weapon for the infantry.

After the war, the Red Army donated several captured Jagdpanzer IVs to the Romanian military, where it continued in service until 1954. Bulgaria also received the Jagdpanzer IV and kept the platform in limited service before converting them into fixed gun emplacements along the Turkish border as part of the Krali Marko Line. Alongside the Panzer IV and StuG III, many Jagdpanzer IVs found their way into the Syrian Army, where they saw combat during the Six-Day War of 1967. Most, however, were destroyed or abandoned in the Golan Heights.

Flakpanzer IV

Of lesser notoriety in the Werhmacht's inventory was the Flakpanzer IV. A mobile air defense gun, the Flakpanzer IV was a generic name given to four different air defense platforms, all of which were based on the Panzer IV chassis. The Wehrmacht units in and around Arracourt possessed the "Wirbelwind" (Whirlwind) variant, armed with quad-mounted 2cm Flak Vierling 38s. Its muzzle velocity and rate of fire were impressive, but its poor fire control systems gave it a low probability of hitting any fast-moving aircraft.

During the early years of World War II, mobile air defense guns were of little concern to the Wehrmacht. After all, the Luftwaffe owned the skies over mainland Europe, and the Allied air forces had yet to gain a toehold on the continent. But as the RAF and U.S. Army Air Forces began to roll back the tide of Nazism, Hitler approved the production and fielding of a series of tactical antiaircraft guns.

One of the latest in the Flakpanzer series, the "Wirbelwind" was a mobile air defense gun that was often adapted to engage ground targets.

When making modifications for the Flakpanzer IV, the standard tank turret was removed and replaced with an open-top gun housing. The open-top design allowed for maximum ventilation for the heavy smoke generated by the four 2cm antiaircraft guns. Like many latter-day air defense vehicles (including the M42 Duster and ZSU 57-2), the Flakpanzers saw extensive use as a ground support vehicle, providing area defense and direct-fire support to infantry units. The Wirbelwind's armament was eventually upgraded to a single-barreled FlaK 43 gun, rebranded as the Flakpanzer IV Ostwind ("East Wind"). Nearly 100 Wirbelwind variants were produced by 1945. A further iteration of the Flakpanzer IV was developed under the codename "Kugelblitz," but only five units were built before the war ended.

Although the Flakpanzer had a short life span and limited role during the war, it did pave the way for an important series of Cold War icons—mobile air defense guns that could keep pace with armored formations. The Western German forces, for example, developed the Flakpanzer Gephard while the Soviets built the renowned ZSU series. The Americans would later develop the M42 Duster, M163 Vulcan Air Defense Systems (VADS), the abortive M247 Sergeant York Division Air Defense (DIVAD) vehicle, and the M6 Bradley Linebacker.

In Profile:
German Armor

Opposite With approximately 6,000 units built, the Panther was among the most ubiquitous German tanks of World War II. The tank was renowned for its firepower and protection; but its mechanical reliability was less than stellar. Crews noted that maintenance of the vehicle was difficult, due in no small part to the interleaved configuration of its road wheels. The Panther performed well in tank-on-tank engagements from standoff distances. In close quarters combat, however, it often fell victim to the American Shermans in the ETO.

Another workhorse among the German armored units was the Flakpanzer IV "Wirbelwind" (German for "Whirlwind"). Based on the Panzer IV tank, the Wirbelwind was a self-propelled anti-aircraft gun. A further development of the Flakpanzer IV, nicknamed "Ostwind" (German for "East Wind") began production in 1944. Only a few dozen Ostwinds were produced before the war ended in 1945, none of which served on the frontlines.

Opposite The Axis equivalent of the M3-series halftrack was the Sonderkraftfahrzeug (Sd.Kfz) 251. Like its Allied counterpart, the Sd.Kfz was primarily an armored personnel carrier, although it served in other capacities on the battlefront. Depicted here is the Schützenpanzerwagen variant, carrying a 75mm KwK37 main gun. This variant of the Sd.Kfz was often nicknamed the "Stummel" (German for "stump").

A Flakpanzer IV similar to the variety used during the final firefights northeast of Arracourt. A further iteration of the Flakpanzer was developed, but production was halted after the Nazis surrendered.

German 1st Army and 5th Panzer Army

During the inaugural days of World War II, there can be little argument that the Wehrmacht conducted its campaigns from a position of strength. By the time hostilities commenced, Germany had already invaded Austria and the Sudetenland. Hitler had rearmed Germany's ailing war machine and put the Reich's best scientists and engineers to work developing the most advanced tanks and aircraft the world had yet seen.

At the forefront of German rearmament was the 1st Army. Activated on August 26, 1939, its primary mission was to defend the Maginot Line. In June 1940, however, while under the command of Army Group C, the 1st Army displaced from its defensive positions and began penetrating the Maginot Line as part of the final blitzkrieg into Paris. After smashing through the remnants of French forces in the Moselle and the Vosges, the 1st Army then secured the so-called "Atlantic Wall" in southwest France, facing the Bay of Biscay.

By this point, however, the 1st Army's subordinate units were none too impressive. Indeed, many of the subordinate divisions were "static divisions"—assigned to coastal defense and lacking even the most basic mobility assets found in other Wehrmacht units. Given the static nature of their mission, these divisions typically had the lowest rung of recruits. Most were older men (35–45 years old), and many had been reassigned to the static mission after to being wounded or having other medical problems. To make matters worse, the 1st Army lost more of its personnel following the Allied invasion of Normandy. In fact, throughout June and July 1944, many of the 1st Army's better units were transferred to Normandy to stem the tide of the Allied advance.

After the Normandy breakout, Allied forces landed in southern France on August 15, 1944, and the German 1st Army began its retreat to the borders of the Reich. The Third and Seventh U.S. Armies made such rapid progress across Western Europe that Hitler was getting nervous. At the time, there were no viable defenses along Germany's western border, from Luxembourg to Switzerland. Thus, Hitler ordered the 1st Army and 19th Army (both of which fell under Army Group G) to make a hasty retreat to the German border regions and reinforce their defenses facing westward.

Getting to the German frontier, however, was no easy task. Because many of the 1st Army's divisions had no motorized or horse-drawn assets, they conducted their march across France using commandeered civilian vehicles and horses. Along the way, French

General Johannes Blaskowitz, commander of Army Group G. Blaskowitz commanded the army group during its retreat across France and during the opening stages of the Lorraine campaign. (Bundesarchiv, Bild 146-2004-004-05 / CC-BY-SA 3.0)

partisans harassed the 1st Army columns as they hobbled across the countryside. The 19th Army, however, fared much worse. Indeed, for most of their retreat, the U.S. Seventh Army was right on their heels.

By the time the 1st Army had settled into its defensive positions in Lorraine, France, its divisions were too weak and disorganized to mount an effective defense of the area. By early September 1944, the 1st Army divisions had been pushed back to the eastern banks of the Moselle River by Patton's vanguard. In response, the German high command dispatched a new corps headquarters to the beleaguered 1st Army along with a handful of new Volksgrenadier divisions. Thus, by the time the battle of Arracourt began, the German 1st Army consisted of little more than a hodgepodge of divisions, most of which were marginally effective or untested in combat. These divisions included (a) the 1st Army's organic divisions that had been eroded during their retreat across France, (b) the semi-intact divisions withdrawn from elsewhere in France, and (c) the newly raised and hastily mobilized Volksgrenadier divisions.

Army Group G's static defenses along the Atlantic Wall. Army Group G's subordinate units were nominally static divisions, trained for coastal defense duty.

In September 1944, the 1st Army's order of battle was as follows:

LXXX Army Corps

- 5th Paratrooper Division

LXXXII Army Corps

- 19th Volksgrenadier Division
- 36th Volksgrenadier Division
- 559th Volksgrenadier Division

XIII SS Corps

- 3d Panzergrenadier Division
- 15th Panzergrenadier Division
- 17th SS Panzergrenadier Division
- 462d Volksgrenadier Division
- 106th Panzer Brigade

The Volksgrenadier units were largely ad hoc formations. Their ranks consisted of lower-quality conscripts, battle-weary veterans, and "excess" personnel from the ailing Luftwaffe and the Kriegsmarine. The Volksgrenadier division had six infantry battalions and relied more on small-arms weaponry than did the conventional infantry units. Although they enjoyed automatic weapons such as the Sturmgewehr 44, and antitank weapons like the Panzerfaust, the Volksgrenadier units often lacked sufficient motorized or mechanized assets.

The Volksgrenadier divisions were a last-ditch effort by Hitler to mobilize every able-bodied male to the frontlines. They were organized by cannibalizing other formations—taking men from training posts, naval units, and/or grounded Luftwaffe squadrons. Like their counterparts in the regular infantry divisions, the Volksgrenadier units differed in quality from one division to the next.

Panzergrenadiers were the mechanized infantrymen of the Wehrmacht. Of the three panzergrenadier divisions assigned to the 1st Army, none was operating at full strength. The 17th SS Panzergrenadier Division, for example, was virtually annihilated during the Normandy campaign, but had recently been reconstituted from elements of the 26th and 27th SS Panzer Divisions. Still, by September 1944, the division was operating at barely 56 percent strength, and had surprisingly few armored assets. Its panzer battalion, for example, had only five assault guns and *two* Panzer III tanks. The other two panzergrenadier divisions were veterans of the Italian campaign but were likewise operating at degraded capacity. The 3d Panzergrenadiers had only four tanks in their panzer battalion, but still had a healthy number of operational Sd.Kfz. halftracks. The tank destroyer battalion had 31 Jagdpanzers, of which only 21 were operational. The 15th Panzergrenadier Division had been formed from remnants of the latter-day 15th Panzer Division that had been destroyed in North Africa, and boasted the most operational tanks, including some 32 Panzer IVs. Their Sd.Kfz. halftracks, however, had slowly diminished, forcing them to rely mostly on commandeered civilian trucks for mobility.

The 1st Army had no organic panzer divisions, but it did have the 106th Panzer Brigade. Later in the Lorraine campaign, however, the 1st Army received elements of the 11th and 21st Panzer Divisions, but neither division was at full strength, and both had taken a tremendous beating from Allied forces prior to arriving in Lorraine.

During Army Group G's retreat across France, they were often harassed and interdicted by French partisans.

The panzer brigades were unique organizations within the Wehrmacht. They began life as independent brigades, but most were eventually absorbed into the panzer and panzergrenadier divisions. The first 10 panzer brigades (101st to 110th) were activated in July 1944, and were created of necessity, rather than any foundational precepts within German Army doctrines. The 106th Panzer Brigade, like its contemporaries, contained a modified panzer battalion and a halftrack panzergrenadier battalion. The panzer battalion had 36 tanks, while the panzergrenadiers had several more Sd.Kfz. halftracks. Although these numbers paled in comparison to Allied units of comparable size, these panzer brigades had more armor capabilities than most panzer divisions at the time.

Because most retreating units lacked mobile assets, many of the Wehrmacht's ground units were forced to use horse-drawn carriages.

The second wave of panzer brigades (111th, 112th, and 113th) were created in early September 1944, as the Allies closed in on Arracourt. All three were sent to the 5th Panzer Army and supported the defense of Lorraine. The organization of the latter panzer brigades was quite different from the previous ten. Each had two Panzer battalions: one battalion of Panzer IV tanks and one battalion of Panther tanks. There were also two Panzergrenadier battalions, an armored reconnaissance company, an engineer company, and an assault gun company.

The panzer brigades were another adaptation by the Wehrmacht, given the realities of the war in France. The panzer brigades were created in two waves. Each wave had a different structure. The first wave contained a modified panzer battalion and a halftrack panzergrenadier battalion. The second wave of panzer brigades each had two panzer battalions: one battalion of Panzer IV tanks and one battalion of Panther tanks. There were also two panzergrenadier battalions, an armored reconnaissance company, an engineer company, and an assault gun company. All of the second-wave panzer brigades fought in Lorraine against the 4th Armored Division and other elements of Patton's Third Army.

Although the Panzer Brigade was an impressive concept on paper, it did not work well in practice. Not surprisingly, many senior panzer commanders were critical of the new

Army Group G lost several pieces of equipment during its retreat into eastern France. Pictured here is a horse-drawn artillery piece, lost in August 1944. The rationale behind the retreat was to reinforce the German border between Luxembourg and Switzerland. From there, Hitler hoped to mount a counteroffensive to push the Allies back into northern and western France.

organization. In fact, General Hasso von Manteuffel, commander of the 5th Panzer Army, proffered the following assessment of his panzer brigades:

> The three independent Panzer brigades [111th, 112th, and 113th] had been newly created by the General Inspector of Panzer Troops and had to be considered improvisations as a result of the general lack of men and materiel. Aside from their rather poor organization, the fighting qualifications of these brigades was particularly handicapped by the fact that the brigades having been activated in different [Military Districts]; they did not have internal coherence whatsoever. Two of the brigade commanders became acquainted with their subordinate commanders only in the railroad unloading area.
>
> In addition, there was a lack of all kinds of materiel and equipment necessary for that type of organization. The brigades' organization in many respects showed signs of improved measures [from the earlier organizations of July 1944]. There

A captured 15cm German howitzer. During Patton's drive to the German border, the Third Army captured several pieces of German equipment. Because supplies and ammunition were running low among the Allied field armies, many of these working German pieces and their ammo stores were commandeered by whichever Allied unit found them. In the case of these German howitzers, American artillery units created entire replacement batteries out of them.

The first independent panzer brigades were equipped with panzergrenadier (mechanized infantry) regiments, operating the Sd.Kfz.-series halftracks. Among these was the Sd.Kfz. 251/9 "Kanonenwagen," armed with a direct-fire 7.5cm gun.

was no artillery … nor was there a coordinating staff for the two armored battalions. The reconnaissance and engineer units were in no way adequate. There was a definite lack of radio equipment. In proportion to the general shortages, the strength and equipment of the armored recovery and repair services were altogether insufficient, although these services are as vitally necessary for the commitment of an armored unit as the very tank itself.

The men could not be trained in combined arms tactics, as they had been activated in several different localities. In spite of numerous examples of individual bravery on the part of men of all ranks, they were unable to live up to what was expected of them. I had my justified doubts as to whether these units would be suitable for any offensive operation with a more far-reaching objective against an enemy such as one [on the Western Front], especially so since the commanders had only limited practical experience in the command of combined arms units on the battlefield.

General Walter Kruger, who had commanded the LVIII Panzer Corps in Lorraine, felt likewise:

Panzer Brigades 111 and 113, like all the Panzer brigades that had been formed, were a makeshift organization. Their combat value was slight. They had originally been intended for commitment in the East [against the Red Army] and had been organized in various garrisons and bases. Their training was just as incomplete as their equipment. They had been given no training as a unit and they had not become accustomed to coordinating their subunits. They were composed by and large of young, inexperienced personnel, together with a small cadre of battle-tested junior officers and NCOs as well as some "barrel scrapings" of overaged men from rear area formations, supply units, and administrative offices.

An American GI stands proudly in front of a knocked-out Panther belonging to the 105th Panzer Brigade.

Even Heinz Guderian fiercely opposed the formation of panzer brigades. Based on his experiences during the blitzkrieg and along the Eastern Front, he knew that it took several months before panzer crews could reach their peak performance. And given the situation of 1944, time was a luxury the Wehrmacht did not have. As Inspector General of Panzer Troops, Guderian favored shipping the new Panther tanks to the existing units that knew how to use them. Not surprisingly, Hitler overruled his general, and the fielding of the panzer brigades went forward.

The latter three of the Wehrmacht's panzer brigades—the 111th, 112th, and 113th—were the keystone formations of the 5th Panzer Army. Originally formed in December 1942, the 5th Panzer Army fought in North Africa before surrendering to Allied forces in Tunisia on May 9, 1943. The 5th Panzer Army was subsequently reformed on August 5, 1944 and fought in the latter stages of the Normandy campaign. Its performance, however, was less than stellar. In fact, the 5th Panzers narrowly escaped destruction in the Falaise Pocket before settling into their new positions in Lorraine.

In September 1944, the 5th Panzer Army's order of battle was as follows:

XXXXVII Panzer Corps[1]

- 21st Panzer Division
- 111th Panzer Brigade
- 112th Panzer Brigade
- 113th Panzer Brigade

---

1   The LVIII Panzer Corps was another corps headquarters assigned to the 5th Panzer Army at this time. At one point during the Lorraine battles, it had operational control of the 111th Panzer Brigade.

Although elements of the 21st Panzer Division had been parceled out to the German 1st Army, the bulk of the division remained under control of the 5th Panzer Army. The 21st Panzer Division, like many of its brethren, had been virtually destroyed during the fighting in Normandy. Most of the division returned to Germany for refitting, although they did leave behind a small cadre to fight within the 1st Army's sector. During the campaigns in and around Arracourt, the commander of Army Group G felt that the 21st Panzer Division was among the least effective units assigned to any of his field armies.

When studying the comparative strength and structure of the American and Wehrmacht divisions, it is clear that the American forces had a better practice of force regeneration. The Germans often kept units in the field until they were no longer effective. When these battered units were brought back into the Fatherland for refitting, they couldn't get enough replacement personnel or equipment to help them reach full strength. This forced many units to consolidate into smaller formations known as battle groups (*Kampfgruppen*) just to retain some level of combat effectiveness. In other cases, divisions would be supplemented by fragmenting formations from other units. Thus, in the final days of the Western Front, there was virtually no unit cohesion among the amalgamated units of the Wehrmacht. The U.S. Army, by contrast, kept their divisions organized as close to their TO&E as possible. American forces were able to accomplish this through a steady stream of men and materiel to the front.

A knocked-out Panther from the 107th Panzer Brigade, September 1944. The panzer brigades were devised as independent, rapidly deployable armored units. Three such panzer brigades were committed to the fighting at Arracourt. In practice, however, the panzer brigades proved to be a disappointment. One of their biggest drawbacks was the lack of organic artillery support.

Throughout the conflict, it often appeared that the Germans had an overwhelming numerical advantage—pitting entire field armies against American divisions. The reality, however, was that the American armored divisions were operating at near full strength while the Wehrmacht was fighting at a degraded capacity. Given the disparity between their force-generation techniques, American and German forces were fighting each other on a more levelled playing field.

Tattered remains of the Luftwaffe contingent in Lorraine, France. By the fall of 1944, the Luftwaffe was no longer a viable air support arm.

In Profile:
General Hasso von Manteuffel

General Hasso von Manteuffel, commander of the 5th Panzer Army.

As commander of the 5th Panzer Army, Manteuffel was, in many ways, Patton's opposing number. Like Patton, he was a veteran of World War I. During the invasion of the Soviet Union in 1941, Manteuffel commanded a panzer battalion within Army Group Center. Two years later, however, he transferred to North Africa where he served in the battle of Tunisia. He was then posted back to the Eastern Front, where he commanded the 7th Panzer Division. In September 1944, he was promoted to General of Panzer Troops and given command of the 5th Panzer Army.

The 11th Panzer Division was the only tank division in Army Group G by the end of August 1944. It had been a rearguard force for the German 19th Army during the retreat toward Alsace. The Panther tank pictured here was lost by the 11th Panzer Division during that retreat. By mid-September, the division had been transferred to support the 5th Panzer Army in and around Arracourt.

| The Strategic Setting

The Allied landings in Normandy marked the beginning of the end for the German Army. On June 6, 1944, the First U.S. Army under General Omar Bradley landed at Omaha and Utah beaches. Bradley's First Army was the only American field army in France until Patton's Third Army arrived the following month.

By the time of the D-Day landings, there were no panzer divisions in the American sector in and around Omaha Beach. In fact, all the panzer divisions were in the British/Canadian sector near Caen. The only mechanized assets opposing American forces at the time was a single panzergrenadier division, along with a few panzer training battalions, some antitank companies, and assault gun battalions.

As Allied forces moved farther inland, American tanks traded very little fire with German armor. Indeed, most of the action during the early days of the Normandy campaign happened in the British sector. During that first month, American tank crews reported

Throughout the first months following the Normandy invasion, most tank kills were caused by field guns, not enemy tanks. Also, many of the early Allied tank-on-tank casualties were suffered by British M4 Sherman crews because they met German armor earlier following the Normandy landings. Moreover, the German tanks tended to perform better against Allied armor when fighting from the defense. The Germans achieved most of their casualties from ambushes.

killing an average of three German tanks per day, while the British reported nearly 14 kills per day. During the same time, most American tank losses came from antitank guns rather than enemy panzers. As American forces moved into the hedgerows in and around Saint-Lô, these one-off armor engagements continued with much the same pattern: American tanks would engage the occasional StuG III or other tank destroyers in the area. When the U.S. Army descended into Saint-Lô proper, however, the Wehrmacht began shifting its panzer forces into the American sector for the first time.

The first qualitative tank battles began that summer when two panzer divisions met the U.S. 9th and 30th Infantry Divisions near the Vire River in July 1944. The ensuing combat cost the panzer forces dearly, with one division losing nearly 30 tanks. Armor operations began reaching fever pitch on July 24, 1944, with the start of Operation *Cobra*. With the

An M4 Sherman from the 712th Tank Battalion moves through the village of Periers. The 712th supported the 90th Infantry Division during its clashes with the Wehrmacht throughout the fall of 1944.

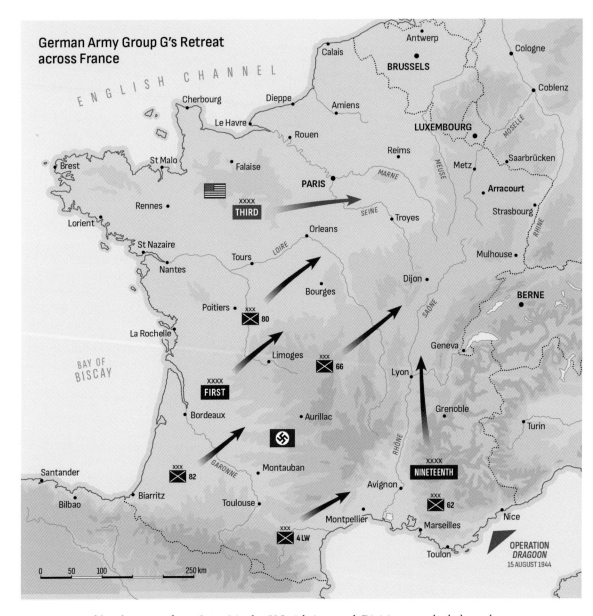

German Army Group G's Retreat across France

intent of breaking out from Saint-Lô, the U.S. 2d Armored Division smashed through the Panzer-Lehr Division. The ensuing attack also routed the 2d SS Panzer Division and remnants of the 17th SS Panzergrenadier Division.

Still, throughout these opening months of the European campaign, tank-on-tank battles were the exception, not the rule. By August 1944, it was clear that most of these early tank engagements were occurring as mobile ambushes. In other words, a Sherman or Panther would lie in wait for an enemy tank, and fire on it before the enemy crew was even cognizant of the threat. It was a nod to the popular adage of armored warfare: "See first, shoot first, hit first."

By the time the 4th Armored Division arrived at the battlefront, Operation *Cobra* was well underway. Still, the division distinguished itself in combat during the Third Army's

Men of the 90th Infantry Division move towards the Moselle River. As one of the prominent natural barriers in the region, the Germans defended it fiercely, trying very hard not to let any American armored or infantry divisions through.

An antitank gun covers an intersection during the fight with the 559th Volksgrenadier Division in early September 1944.

American GIs inspect knocked-out German halftracks. Although the Sd.Kfz. 251 was an "armored" vehicle, it was comparatively thin-skinned. At best, it could only stop the normal variety of Allied small arms. The Sd.Kfz. was often an easy target for American tanks and antitank guns.

By fall 1944, the Luftwaffe began suffering more from logistical problems than from enemy aircraft. Incapable of maintaining a two-front war, the Luftwaffe began grounding many of its planes as their units simply ran out of fuel and spare parts. As such, the German forces in Western Europe often lacked air support. The Americans, however, were dominating the skies over France and Germany. To this end, the P-47 Thunderbolt and other close air support assets became critical force multipliers for the American ground forces.

drive to the River Seine. Seizing the Seine, Patton argued, would help secure the Allies' foothold in Normandy and facilitate enveloping the local Wehrmacht ground units. During Patton's advance to the Seine, the 4th Armored Division encountered few panzers, as they were still concentrated farther north. Several other German units, meanwhile, had been trapped in the Falaise Pocket between Caen and Chambois.

The Germans, for their part, were in a desperate scramble to defend the western borders of the Fatherland and prevent the Allies from penetrating the Reich. The Normandy campaign had taken a heavy toll on the western contingent of the Wehrmacht, and Hitler was determined to defend the border stretching from Luxembourg to Switzerland. His plan of action along the western border was unofficially known as the "Vosges panzer offensive" because much of the action was anticipated to take place in the Vosges Mountains near Arracourt. This area also included the Moselle and Rhine rivers and the legacy Westwall defenses.

German military planners could see the strategic importance of the area. For if the Americans crossed the Moselle River, it would put them within striking distance of Mannheim, Stuttgart, and Frankfurt. This, in turn, would allow the Americans to envelop Germany's industrial center in the Ruhr region. If either area was lost to the Allies, it would severely impact what little industrial resources Germany had left.

Traditionally, these industrial heartlands had been protected by the Westwall—a series of fortifications that had guarded the Franco-German border. By 1944, however, much of the Westwall had fallen into disrepair; its fortifications had been cannibalized and redirected to the Atlantic Wall as a safeguard against the Allied invasion. But this reallocation of defense resources would cost the Germans dearly as the Allies moved into Alsace-Lorraine.

As the German 1st Army and 5th Panzer Army took up positions in Lorraine, Hitler ordered a revitalization of the Westwall positions in September 1944. But it was too little, too late. Indeed, by this time, none of the frontline forces had the wherewithal to stop the oncoming Third Army. And even the best static defenses on the Westwall could be outflanked by a highly determined mechanized force.

*

Arracourt itself is located in the heart of Lorraine, France—among the aforementioned regional landmarks of the Vosges Mountains and Moselle River. The first major tank skirmishes in Lorraine began on September 8, 1944, in the town of Mairy.

By this time, the German 1st Army was in poor shape, owing to its battered formations and frequent leadership changes at the higher echelons. To make matters worse, the 1st Army had lost one of its best mechanized units, the 15th Panzergrenadier Division, when Hitler ordered it to be transferred to the 19th Army in preparation for the Vosges panzer

American GIs from the 5th Infantry Division prepare to cross the Moselle River.

offensive. Hitler did, however, authorize a temporary transfer of the 106th Panzer Brigade on the condition that its actions be approved by the Führer himself.

On August 31, from the German side of the lines, it appeared that the U.S. Third Army had halted near Verdun to prepare for an assault through Luxembourg. In reality, however, the Third Army had halted on account of fuel shortages. But whatever the reason for Patton's halt, the Germans decided to take advantage of it. The current 1st Army commander, General Kurt von der Chevallerie, proposed using the 106th Panzer Brigade as the vanguard of an attack against Patton's forces near Metz. Under this plan, elements of the 15th Panzergrenadier Division and 19th Volksgrenadier Division would reinforce the 106th during its attack.

Patton, meanwhile, continued grappling with chronic fuel shortages. For the first week of September, he had requested 4.7 million gallons of fuel but received only 1.8 million—barely enough to move his divisions for a day and a half. His 3d Cavalry Group, however, had managed to siphon some 4,000 gallons from an abandoned Luftwaffe depot, thus giving

Crossing the Moselle River was no easy task. Many of the pre-existing French-built forts (like Fort Driant, pictured here) provided excellent redoubts for German artillery. The Allies eventually gained the upper hand by bombing and occupying many of these outpost forts.

With ammunition shortages growing at an ever-increasing rate, American troops began to turn the Germans' own 8.8cm guns against them.

the recon squadrons enough fuel to probe the German lines for two more days. In fact, it was these probing attacks that prompted the 106th Panzer Brigade's attack of September 8.

For this opening skirmish in Lorraine, it seemed that the 106th Panzer Brigade would have the upper hand. It was commanded by one of the finest tank commanders in Germany: Colonel Dr Franz Bäke. Its ranks included battle-hardened veterans from the Eastern Front and this new brigade was equipped with the latest and greatest in German armor. However, for the 106th Panzer Brigade, the experience of its men and the quality of its equipment could not compensate for its hasty fielding and lack of crew cohesion. Even with a cadre of combat veterans, it would take several weeks and/or months to reach the level of crew synchronicity needed to perform adequately in combat.

Directly in the path of the 106th Panzer Brigade were the men of the U.S. 90th Infantry Division (the "Tough 'Ombres"), one of many divisions under the Third Army's jurisdiction. The 90th Division, however, had one of the worst reputations in the ETO. Its combat performance during the Normandy campaign had been so abysmal that army planners had considered disbanding the division and parceling out its men to other outfits with better reputations. However, it was soon discovered that systemic poor leadership had been the root of the problem. By September 1944, after purging and replacing several key leaders, the 90th Division had transformed itself into a highly effective combat unit. Attached to the division was the 712th Tank Battalion along with the 607th Tank Destroyer Battalion. On the morning of September 8, the 90th Infantry Division and its combined elements were poised to give the 106th Panzer Brigade a rude awakening.

The predawn attack perpetrated by the 106th ended in disaster. Indeed, it was so poorly executed that the Americans thought the enemy had been conducting an administrative march and accidentally stumbled into the Allied sector. By the end of the day, the 106th

Panzer Brigade had been virtually destroyed. Battle damage assessments vary from source to source, but there is little question that the young panzer brigade suffered a catastrophic defeat. One report claims as many as 54 Sd.Kfz. 251 halftracks were lost, along with 30 tanks and more than 100 wheeled vehicles destroyed. By contrast, the Americans lost only *two* M4 Sherman tanks.

The debacle with the 106th Panzer Brigade was a function of poor planning and improper execution. The Panther tanks were effective against Allied Shermans, but these crews were less adept at confronting dispersed infantry. The Panther was, of course, technologically superior, but its advanced construction mattered little in the face of American artillery. As was common throughout the ETO, artillery was the most casualty-producing weapon on the ground, hence its nickname: "King of Battle." The 106th Panzer Brigade, meanwhile, had *zero* artillery support. Thus, it came as no surprise that the Americans' indirect fire would give them a tactical edge. In fact, artillery was the one combat arm in which the Americans had unquestioned superiority over the Wehrmacht.

This defeat of the 106th Panzer Brigade, however, illustrated the organizational deficiencies within the Wehrmacht's formations and the operational myopia of its planners. The panzer brigade's failure further disrupted the tenuous balance of forces defending the western borders and paved the way for the Third Army's thrust into the Vosges region.

*

After fighting their way through Epinal during the second week of September, Patton's Third Army had arrived at the edge of the Moselle River—the last physical barrier before the German frontier. Patton was certain that he could cross the Rhine by October 1, but the battered German units were determined to halt his advance at any cost. In fact, the Third Army's arrival along the Moselle had reoriented the focus of the Vosges panzer offensive to the Moselle region.

For the first time since the invasion of Normandy, the Germans now appeared to be operating from a position of strength. Ironically, as they occupied their positions near the Moselle River, they were assisted by the region's infrastructure—a network of 19th-century French- and German-built forts. Each of the old fortifications had been built specifically to halt river crossings. And the three corps units within Patton's Third Army (XII, XV, and XX) met considerable resistance while trying to cross the Moselle. Near Dornot, for example, a battalion from the 5th Infantry Division (XX Corps) tried to establish a bridgehead but were repelled by the 17th SS Panzergrenadier Division and German artillery fire from nearby Fort Driant. The U.S. 7th Armored Division had similar difficulty crossing the Moselle, courtesy

Much of the Wehrmacht's Atlantic defenses were manned by so-called "combat rejects," older men who could not withstand the normal wear and tear of everyday soldiering, or those who had medical problems. These soldiers constituted the Wehrmacht's static infantry divisions, whose demonstrable purpose was coastal defense. However, as the Allies broke out from Normandy, and invaded southern France in August 1944, these static divisions scrambled across France to form a defensive position along the German border.

of German artillery fire. The German batteries continued harassing American troops until they were overwhelmed during the American Operation *Thunderbolt* later in September.

With the XX Corps units tied down in the face of enemy fire, Patton turned his attention to XII Corps under General Manton Eddy. The XII Corps divisions were situated near the city of Nancy, the historic capital of Lorraine. Because the terrain surrounding Nancy did not lend itself to an easy river crossing, Eddy elected to stage his crossings at simultaneous points farther north and south to facilitate encircling the German defenders.

On September 5, 1944, elements of the 80th Infantry Division began crossing the Moselle River near Pont-a-Mousson. However, they were soon beaten back by the 3d Panzergrenadier Division. Undeterred, the 80th Division shifted its attention farther south to Dieulouard, but here again, they encountered stiff German resistance. The 29th Panzergrenadier Regiment, supported by a battery of StuG III assault guns, pushed the Americans back some 100 yards. However, the 80th Division, alongside the 702d Tank Battalion, regained the initiative and crushed the German counterattack. Almost simultaneously, the 35th Infantry Division moved to seize river crossings south of Nancy. One battalion gained several bridgeheads

The 8th Tank Battalion, Combat Command B, 4th Armored Division, negotiates crossing points along the Bayon Canal as they approach Arracourt.

When Combat Command B crossed the Bayon Canal, the Wehrmacht responded with a local counterattack. The 15th Panzergrenadier Division led the charge with their Panzer IV tanks. One of these tanks, seen here in the background, was knocked out by an American Sherman.

Captured members of the 3d Panzergrenadier Division march through Dieulouard on September 13, 1944. Combat Command A had used the bridgehead at Dieulouard as a springboard for their drive into Arracourt. The panzergrenadiers fought tenaciously to keep the 4th Armored Division from crossing through Dieulouard. However, within a few hours, Combat Command A had plowed through the Germans' position.

on September 10, but another battalion was overwhelmed by the Germans' coordinated air and artillery attacks. Sensing that the situation needed an armored thrust, General Eddy dispatched the 4th Armored Division to Nancy.

The "Name Enough" Division's orders were simple: concentrate maximum firepower into the pockets of enemy resistance and exploit any secured bridgeheads. Combat Command B (CCB) spearheaded the drive to the Bayon Canal and, within hours, had crossed a bridgehead to link up with a regiment from the 35th Infantry Division near Lorney. The 15th Panzergrenadier Division, meanwhile, attempted a counterattack but their efforts were promptly crushed.

Local German commanders negotiate the surrender of 20,000 German 1st Army troops trapped by overlapping elements of the Third and Seventh Armies, September 1944. As the American field armies continued their drive to the border, many trapped units surrendered rather than face annihilation. This, in turn, robbed Hitler of any residual forces for the Reichland border counteroffensives.

Captain Brady, commander of Company A, 35th Tank Battalion, 4th Armored Division, during the fighting at Lunéville.

Meanwhile, the 4th Armored Division's commander, Major General John Wood, ordered Combat Command A (CCA) to cross the river at Dieulouard and link up with CCB to complete the encirclement of Nancy proper. With a troop of M8 Greyhounds leading the charge, CCA's forward elements reached the western banks of the river by 4:00 AM while elements of the 80th Division were still fighting on the eastern side. The M8 armored cars fought their way through the German infantry but were beaten back by a dug-in battery of StuG III assault guns.

Despite that minor setback, however, CCA doubled down and drove forward. With Creighton Abrams's 37th Tank Battalion leading the way, the combat command plowed through the German positions. By the end of the day on September 12, CCA had destroyed nearly 100 enemy vehicles and had nearly completed the encirclement of Nancy. According to the division logs: "The rapid drive of CCA through enemy lines had so disrupted enemy forces that small groups have been apprehended wandering, almost aimlessly, through their bivouac areas." In fact, the 4th Armored Division's breakthrough at Moselle had been so successful that Hitler himself had taken notice. The 4th Armored Division was now his priority target for the Vosges panzer offensive.

*

Although the Americans had dictated the tempo for most of the Western European campaign, it appeared that the upcoming battle at Arracourt was about to put the combatants on a more equal footing. Indeed, each side would be going into the battle with its own advantages and disadvantages. The Americans still held the initiative, and the Germans were still on the defensive. With the amalgamation of local forces, however, the Germans had numerical superiority. The panzer units based in Lorraine were operating Panzer IVs and the newer Panther tanks.

Artillery was the one dimension where American ground forces had unquestioned superiority over the Wehrmacht. Panzer brigades had no organic artillery, and the legacy Wehrmacht units had mostly towed artillery pieces. The Americans, by contrast had a mobile fleet of armored self-propelled guns, and forward observers who could keep pace with the armored formations. Moreover, the Americans often captured the abandoned German artillery pieces and added them to their own battalions, forming additional batteries to supplement organic American guns.

Although the Panzer IV was comparable to the Sherman, the Panther was a significant threat. It was practically light years ahead of the Sherman in terms of its armor protection and firepower. Its frontal armor was impervious against the standard Soviet and American tank guns. Meanwhile, its own 7.5cm main gun had more stopping power than most Allied tanks, and it could easily penetrate any point on the Sherman from ranges beyond 1,000 yards. The Panther's side armor, however, was relatively weak.

Thus, if a Sherman wished to knock out a Panther, it would have to do so by engaging it from the sides or rear where the armor was weakest. This necessitated the use of close-in fighting tactics, which played to the Sherman's advantage—the Panther was not optimized for close-quarter combat. And although the Panther had superior firepower in terms of brute strength, the M4 Sherman had a better fire control system. Indeed, the Sherman gunners had *two* sights—a coaxial telescopic sight and a regular periscope. The periscope gave the gunner a wider field of vision. This, in turn, afforded better situational awareness and faster target acquisition. The Panther gunners, by contrast, had only a telescopic sight, which gave them a limited view of the battlespace. This also forced them to rely on their tank commanders for target identification and higher-level situational awareness. In fact, according to one postwar analysis, whenever the Panther's commander identified a target, it would take nearly 20–30 seconds for his gunner to confirm and engage. "This delay," said the report, "which is significantly greater than that of the Sherman, stems from the absence of a periscope for the gunner."

The Sherman had another advantage over the Panther in terms of its traversing capabilities. Both tanks had power traversing, but the hydraulics aboard the Panther were slaved to the main engine. Thus, the turret hydraulics could only be engaged if the tank's power output was not otherwise supporting another function. The hydraulics aboard the Sherman, however, operated on its own motor, thus allowing more flexibility of use. Aboard the Panther, the turret itself was not well balanced, which made the traversing sluggish if the tank were on an incline surface.

The Panther had better off-road handling, but its fuel consumption lagged behind the Sherman. In fact, Heinz Guderian had remarked that: "the large fuel consumption of Panthers makes it necessary to consider whether the mission is worth the cost." To make matters worse, amidst the dwindling fuel supply, the German Army was forced to fill its Panthers and Panzer IVs with lower-grade fuel, which degraded the engine's performance in both vehicles. The true Achilles heel of the Panther, however, was its faulty transmissions and final drive assemblies. Like much of the tank itself, the transmission was over-engineered, and would suffer premature stripping in third gear. The final drive assembly would often break down at less than half of its rated mileage. Indeed, during the Normandy campaign,

3-inch antitank gun crews in action on the approach to Metz.

Negotiating the river crossing at Port-sur-Seille. Sights such as these were common throughout Lorraine, wherein combat engineers could establish a bridgehead, with varying degrees of difficulty based on enemy harassment, to accommodate smooth passage of armored vehicles. Tank crews vastly preferred this method of crossing instead of tactical fording.

the Allies discovered that nearly half of the abandoned Panther tanks had faulty drive assemblies.

Overall, the Panzer IV had better reliability than the Panther, but even the Sherman was more reliable than the fourth-iteration Panzer. Throughout the spring and summer of 1944, Panzer IV units averaged an operational readiness rate of around 50 percent. The 4th Armored Division, meanwhile, kept its Shermans at a 99 percent readiness rate throughout most of the campaign. Even at its worst, the "Name Enough" Divison had a 92 percent readiness rate.

Still, the Sherman lagged behind the panzers in terms of its armor protection and brute-strength firepower. The M4- and M4A3-variant Shermans in Lorraine carried the 75mm and 76mm main guns, respectively. Tank crewmen preferred the 75mm gun as they deemed it more versatile than the 76mm variant, which had been optimized for tank-on-tank engagements. But whichever caliber they used, neither gun could match the muzzle velocity or the penetrating power of the German tanks. The latter-day Panthers, for example, had a muzzle velocity of 925 meters per second and could penetrate up to 129mm of armor. The M4A3 Sherman, by contrast, had a muzzle velocity of only 792 meters per second and could barely penetrate 96mm of armor.

But what the Sherman lacked in pure metrics, the crews compensated for with superior metaphysics. For example, there can be little question that, by 1944, the American tank units had better training and better crew synchronicity than their counterparts in the Wehrmacht. The ailing logistics and lack of time had taken their toll on the panzer crews' combat effectiveness. American tactics also helped mitigate the German's armored advantage. The Americans had devised a number of innovative tactics to overcome the Panther's brute strength. One such tactic was to hit the Panther with a white phosphorus round. Some crews would mistake the smoke for an internal fire and jump out of the tank, whereupon they'd be cut down by American machine-gun fire. Other crews would be forced out of the tank because the bitter smoke would be drawn into the turret through the tank's ventilator. But even if the smoke failed to eject an enemy tank crew, it would nonetheless obscure their vision long enough for the Shermans to maneuver along the flanks or rear, lining up the 75mm gun for a kill shot. This tactic was the standard operating procedure in Combat Command A of the 4th Armored Division. Situational awareness also stood in the Americans' favor. Aside from the aforementioned periscope mount, the American tanks maintained better communication via FM radio. The German Panthers, meanwhile, were still using AM radios, which were more susceptible to interference. Apart from their superior radios, the American armored units often kept tank-mounted artillery fire supports teams and forward air controllers. These tank-mounted observers could keep pace with the M4 maneuvers and call real-time artillery and air strikes on German positions. The Germans, by this point, were lacking viable artillery support and the Luftwaffe had been stretched beyond its capacity to function in a credible air support role.

| The Battle

The battle of Arracourt began, in earnest, on the outskirts of nearby Lunéville on September 15, 1944. The breakthrough along the Moselle had prompted Hitler to refocus the Vosges panzer offensive units onto a new objective: destroying the 4th Armored Division. The Germans planned to use Lunéville as the launch point for their counterattack against Patton's frontline forces.

Troop C from the 42d Cavalry Squadron, 2d Cavalry Group, sent two of its recon platoons (one mounted, the other dismounted) into the city on September 15. The mounted platoon of M8 Greyhounds came under fire as it approached the village. One of the Allied crewmen recalled:

> Something gave the M8 a helluva jolt and the driver looked at me and said he couldn't steer anymore. We climbed out and saw that an 88 [German antitank gun] had blown off our right front wheel, and we immediately dived into the ditch alongside the road. We were no more than on the ground when a second 88 drilled the car right through the middle. After that, we just did what the rest of the dismounted men were doing—we ran!

General Manteuffel (left) cheerfully confers with his fellow officers even as the situation grows more dire, September 1944.

A tank commander from the 111th Panzer Brigade asks a senior lieutenant for directions on the approach to Lunéville.

American GIs drive past the wreckage of a Panzer IV near Lunéville, September 20, 1944.

They had just been engaged by a battle group from the 15th Panzergrenadier Division. These panzergrenadiers had occupied Lunéville but their hold on the town was tenuous at best.

Meanwhile, other elements from the 42d Cavalry maneuvered around the city. Troop A, for example, went east of town to another nearby village where they destroyed a Nazi ammunition dump. Other troops gathered reliable field intelligence indicating a heavy armored presence in and around Lunéville.

As such, the 42d Cavalry requested armor support.

The 35th Tank Battalion from Combat Command Reserve (CCR), 4th Armored Division answered the call, sending a handful of tanks to affect a deliberate attack on Lunéville. The 15th Panzergrenadier Division, meanwhile, brought in a handful of new tanks and antitank guns to strengthen their own positions.

The attack on Lunéville began at 1:30 PM on September 16, forcing the panzergrenadiers to withdraw into the neighboring towns of Forêt de Parroy and Forêt de Mondon. Following the enemy's withdrawal, the remainder of CCR, 4th Armored Division (along with companies from the 704th Tank Battalion and 10th Armored Infantry Battalion) arrived in Lunéville by 8:00 PM and set up defensive positions within the town proper. The following day, September 17, the panzergrenadiers led a counterattack into Lunéville, which did not end well for the Germans. Indeed, the panzergrenadiers lost two Sd.Kfz. 251 halftracks, 75 men killed, with an additional 80 men captured. The Americans lost only one M4 Sherman, two men killed, and 15 wounded. Later that evening, the 15th Panzergrenadier Division infiltrated back into the city, occupying its southeastern fringes while most of the American elements remained on the northern side of town. Although the panzergrenadiers had taken a terrific beating at the hands of the 4th Armored Division and 42d Cavalry, the reality was that neither the Germans nor the Americans had enough dismounts to decisively "occupy" Lunéville.

Meanwhile, General Hasso von Manteuffel, commander of the 5th Panzer Army, knew that the situation was deteriorating. Hitler was ordering all mechanized forces in the area to attack the incoming 4th Armored Division, but Manteuffel knew that his panzer contingents weren't ready. Moreover, Colonel-General Johannes Blaskowitz, commander of Army Group G, knew that the Führer wouldn't tolerate any further delays. Thus, Manteuffel was ordered to attack the Americans with whatever assets he had available. The panzer-based counteroffensive would thus begin on Monday, September 18, 1944. The first wave of the counterattack would involve the 15th Panzergrenadier Division, supported by elements from the 111th Panzer Brigade and 21st Panzer Division.

As American forces approached the Moselle River, the Germans took up positions along a series of 18th- and 19th-century-era forts on the French–German border. These legacy forts had been built for the purpose of frontier defense during the days of linear formations, muskets, and cannonballs. Although primitive by 20th-century standards, these forts were built to withstand the ravages of siege warfare, and offered excellent redoubts for German artillery and forward observers.

At 6:00 AM, two battle groups from the 111th Panzer Brigade ran into the 42d Cavalry's screen line southeast of Lunéville. The vanguard Panthers stumbled upon an outpost of M8 Greyhound armored cars. Not surprisingly, the M8's 37mm gun was ineffective against the Panther's frontal armor. The squadron's M7 Howitzer Motor Carriages (HMCs) were soon dispatched to provide direct-fire support, but even their heavier armament was likewise useless against the Panthers. Within moments, half of the HMCs had been destroyed. Outgunned, the mounted cavalry outposts were ordered to withdraw back into Lunéville. The panzer battle groups gave chase but were slowed by an aggressive defense organized by the squadron's dismounted troops. While holding back the oncoming panzers, the 42d Cavalry radioed CCR, advising them of the situation. In response, the 35th Tank Battalion set up a defensive perimeter northwest of Lunéville. Meanwhile, a platoon of M18 Hellcats from the 704th Tank Destroyers along with a platoon of Shermans from the 35th Tank Battalion settled into the southeastern side of town. This outpost of M18s and M4s soon encountered four Panther tanks, the spearhead of the 111th Panzer Brigade's attack. The M18s promptly destroyed two of the leading Panthers, whereupon the other two Panthers beat a hasty retreat.

One the M18 vehicle commanders, Lieutenant Richard Buss, identified another Panther at a range of 300 yards. The tank was moving parallel to their position, thus giving the M18

General John Wood (seated), commander of the 4th Armored Division, confers with Colonel Bruce Clarke, the commander of Combat Command A, as the unit approaches Arracourt proper.

Creighton Abrams's tank sports some tactical camouflage near Arracourt.

The M18 Hellcat featured prominently in the battle at Arracourt, knocking out several enemy tanks, but also losing many of its own.

a clear shot at the Panther's vulnerable side armor. Buss then ordered his wingman, Sergeant Romek, to maneuver his own M18 into position for a kill shot. Romek, in turn, directed his gunner to liquidate the target. After two well-placed shots, the Panther ground to a halt. Although it was a confirmed kill, and a definitive showcase of the M18's destructive power, Buss admitted that he was underwhelmed by the explosion. He had expected a much more brilliant fireworks display than the one he witnessed. But such was the nature of armored combat. Often, the explosions from real-life vehicle kills did not match the spectacular displays seen in training films or Hollywood pictures.

But the situation was about to grow more intense.

Indeed, 30 additional Panthers were making their way down the road into Lunéville and the dismounted panzergrenadiers had begun swarming the area. Because the M18 Hellcat lacked any type of defensive machine gun, the vehicle would be of little use against the oncoming horde of infantry. Thus, the M18s withdrew back into town, but not before confirming nine enemy tanks destroyed.

As the Germans descended onto Lunéville, CCR and the 2d Cavalry Group sprang into action. CCR brought forward its artillery battalions and directed fire against the incoming waves of the 15th Panzergrenadier Division and 111th Panzer Brigade. The artillery barrage, which rained fire on the Germans at key road junctures leading into town, caused staggering losses to the Panzer IV and Panther formations. Battle damage assessments estimated as many as 10 Panzer IVs and 12 Panthers were destroyed during the fire missions.

A few hours later, CCR radioed for reinforcements. Task Force Hunter (from CCA, 4th Armored Division) answered the call and departed at 1:00 PM in a mad dash to Lunéville. Task

A Panther tank prepares for action near Arracourt.

Panther tanks of the 111th Panzer Brigade take up positions in Arracourt.
(Above: Bundesarchiv, Bild 101I-301-1955-18A / Kurth / CC-BY-SA 3.0)

Panther tanks of the 111th Panzer Brigade take up positions in Arracourt.
(Above: Bundesarchiv, Bild 101I-301-1955-22 / Kurth / CC-BY-SA 3.0)

River crossings were arguably the most dangerous aspect of ground warfare in the ETO. The Germans had already destroyed a number a number of bridges during their retreat across France, hoping to impede the Allies' movements. In many respects, they were successful. But even crossing an intact bridgehead presented numerous challenges. For example, the traveling forces would be canalized along the thoroughfare and become more vulnerable to enemy artillery.

Force Hunter was an amalgamated, combined-arms task force consisting of three maneuver companies and one artillery battery. The participating units were Company A, 37th Tank Battalion; Company B, 53d Armored Infantry Battalion; Company C, 704th Tank Destroyer Battalion; and Battery C, 94th Armored Field Artillery Battalion. With their combined direct- and indirect-fire assets, the Americans successfully pushed the 111th Panzer Brigade out of Lunéville by nightfall.

Absent from the fighting that day was the 113th Panzer Brigade. Due to several miscommunications amongst the fragmented chain of command, Manteuffel thought that his forces had recaptured Lunéville by mid-afternoon on September 18. He thus ordered the 113th to stand down and occupy Foret de Parroy for a planned follow-up attack the next day. By the time Manteuffel realized the true situation, however, it was too late to redirect the panzer brigade back towards Lunéville—the Americans had already occupied the town and their artillery screen would smash any attempt at a panzer breakthrough. Thus, Manteuffel had prosecuted the counterattack on Lunéville with less than half the forces he had intended to employ.

Soldiers of the 211th Panzergrenadier Regiment mount a Panther tank in the village of Bures on September 20 in preparation for the attack on Arracourt. (Bundesarchiv, Bild 101I-301-1955-15 / Kurth / CC-BY-SA 3.0)

Knocked-out tanks near Rechicourt, where much of the Arracourt fighting had spilled over.

A pair of knocked-out Panthers at Rechicourt.

General Patton (right) meets with General John Wood (left) to discuss future operations.

Sergeant Kenneth Boyer of Company B, 37th Tank Battalion sits atop his M4 Sherman on September 26, 1944. This photo was taken during the battalion's brief rest period before the final German attacks of September 27–29.

Grenadiers show off their Panzerfaust rockets while seated on the back deck of a Panther from the 111th Panzer Brigade during a lull in the fighting at Arracourt. (Bundesarchiv, Bild 101I-301-1955-21 / Kurth)

A Panther from the 111th Panzer Brigade moves out from Bures towards Arracourt on the morning of September 20, 1944. (Bundesarchiv, Bild 101I-301-1954-06 / Kurth / CC-BY-SA 3.0)

The 191st Field Artillery tows its howitzers en route to its battery emplacement. The 191st provided fire support to the tank crews and armored infantrymen during the fighting in and around Arracourt proper.

The skirmishes in and around Lunéville continued until September 19. In four days of combat, American forces counted more than 1,000 enemy soldiers killed or captured, and at least 13 enemy tanks destroyed. In fact, the German counterattack on Lunéville had been so poorly executed that Patton and his subordinate commanders thought it was little more than a local action—neither Patton nor his intelligence staff knew that the fight in Lunéville had been the vanguard action for a larger offensive involving the 5th Panzer Army. Thus, he ordered the 4th Armored Division to prepare for combat as the spearhead element of the final push to the German border. CCR and Task Force Hunter, after being relieved in place by the 6th Armored Division, rejoined 4th Armored in preparation for the new attack. The plan for September 19 was simple: attack east and penetrate the borders of the Third Reich. CCA would launch from its staging area, attacking northeast from Arracourt towards the River Saar, which formed part of the border between Germany and France.

Manteuffel, meanwhile, realizing that his fight for Lunéville had been in vain, ordered all remaining units to prepare for an attack towards Arracourt. However, one of his subordinate corps commanders protested, claiming that the available forces were not yet ready to launch a counterattack of that magnitude. But Manteuffel had little choice in the matter. The pressure from Berlin and Manteuffel's higher headquarters at Army Group G had forced him into a premature action. He knew that the 4th Armored Division was congregating near Arracourt, but his reconnaissance assets were unable to give him an adequate picture of the enemy's disposition. To make matters worse, the Eastern Front veterans within his ranks had a strong tendency to go "rogue" and launch their own low-level attacks without proper reconnaissance. With these factors combined, Manteuffel's chances for success in the forthcoming attack were slim to none.

The 111th Panzer Brigade begins its attack on Arracourt. (Bundesarchiv, Bild 101I-301-1955-28 / Kurth)

Nevertheless, Manteuffel's plan was for the 5th Panzer Army to attack at dawn on September 19 with the 113th Panzer Brigade in the lead. The 113th would attack north along the Metz–Strasbourg road while the 111th would attack west towards Arracourt. Their objective for September 19 was to overrun the American positions and link up with the 553d Volksgrenadier Division north of Nancy. In the path of these two advancing panzer brigades stood CCA of the 4th Armored Division. CCA had settled around Arracourt with the 25th Cavalry Squadron providing a screen line to the north and east.

Although the Germans and Americans fought tenaciously, both were hamstrung by ongoing logistical problems. Fuel shortages seemed to be one of the most recurring themes during the opening days of the ETO. Patton's forces were halted more than once due to fuel shortages. The panzers, meanwhile, were forced to use lower-grade gasoline, which degraded engine performance and longevity.

*

At dawn on September 19, the area surrounding Arracourt was covered by a dense, low-lying fog. Early morning rain and fog were typical at that time of year and would limit visibility for the combatants on both sides. The terrain itself, however, was almost ideal for tank warfare—flat, agricultural land with intermittent rolling hills. The hills weren't very high; but in a flat and featureless battlespace, a rise of even a few meters is militarily significant. Indeed, many of these hills provided excellent redoubts with clear visibility for several hundred meters in any direction.

Throughout the previous night, the 113th Panzer Brigade had moved into their designated assembly area near Ommeray, but their movements were detected by a company from the 37th Tank Battalion, who radioed the 94th Field Artillery for a fire mission. The howitzers happily obliged, raining fire onto the German bivouac during the predawn hours of September 19. The panicking Germans quickly adjusted their positions.

Shortly after daybreak, and through the dense screen of the morning fog, the German advance parties began exfiltrating from their assembly areas. Many of these advance parties were interdicted by the 37th Tank Battalion near Lezey along the Metz–Strasbourg road. Initial interrogations with German POWs revealed that a column of nearly two dozen tanks—Panthers and Panzer IVs—were headed towards Lezey.

The battle of Arracourt began that morning with a firefight involving a platoon of M5A1 light tanks from Company D, 37th Tank Battalion and the forward elements of the 113th Panzer Brigade. The M5A1s were conducting screen-line operations at the easternmost edge of CCA's position. That platoon engaged and destroyed an enemy halftrack along with an unspecified truck. A few moments later, however, five Panther tanks emerged from behind the burning vehicles. The platoon radioed the situation to their battalion commander, Creighton Abrams, who subsequently ordered their withdrawal—these light tanks were a screening force; they were not intended to fight toe-to-toe against enemy armor. In any event, there was no way an M5 Stuart could stand against a fully loaded Panther tank.

Because the 111th Panzer Brigade lacked the Sd.Kfz. halftracks or sufficient troop-carrier trucks, the dismounts often rode into battle on the panzers themselves. (Bundesarchiv, Bild 101I-301-1955-23 / Kurth)

A Panther tank from the 111th Panzer Brigade moves past a road marker sign outside the town of Bures near Arracourt.

An M4 Sherman tank from the 37th Tank Battalion prepares for action.

Almost simultaneously, another German column was spotted by a platoon from Company C, 37th Tank Battalion. Equipped with the heavier and more capable M4 Sherman, this platoon fired on the advancing German column. The platoon leader, Lieutenant Smith, radioed his company commander, Captain Lamison, warning him of the Germans' approach. As the Panthers emerged from the fog, Smith's platoon opened fire, destroying at least two enemy tanks in the opening volley. The remaining Panthers pulled back just as Captain Lamison dispatched another platoon of M4s to a nearby ridgeline to cut off the Germans' escape. In the ensuing firefight, four additional Panthers were destroyed by flanking shots from the Company C Shermans. It was here along the ridgeline that the Americans used the terrain to their advantage. The American M4s had disappeared behind the reverse slope of the ridgeline. Moments later, these M4s reemerged at a different point along the ridge, knocking out the four remaining Panthers in the column.

Even had the Germans pursued the Americans up the ridge, their Panther tanks would have been at a disadvantage due to the comparative weight of the turret. Throughout the battle of Arracourt, the Panther's heavy turret and its traversing issues put it at a disadvantage. In fact, one American tank company commander remarked that: "Almost all our losses were to tanks or [assault] guns in emplaced positions. Unless our tanks ran directly into prepared fire, they could get off four or five rounds before the Germans could traverse their turrets." These traversing issues were amplified when the Panther operated on an inclined surface, such as the undulating hills or ridgelines in the vicinity of Arracourt.

As CCA became aware of the firefights erupting in the 37th Tank Battalion sector, they dispatched a platoon from Company C, 704th Tank Destroyer Battalion to establish blocking positions on Hill 246 approximately 800 yards north of Rechicourt-la-Petite. This would allow them to interdict any remaining elements of the 113th Panzer Brigade, should

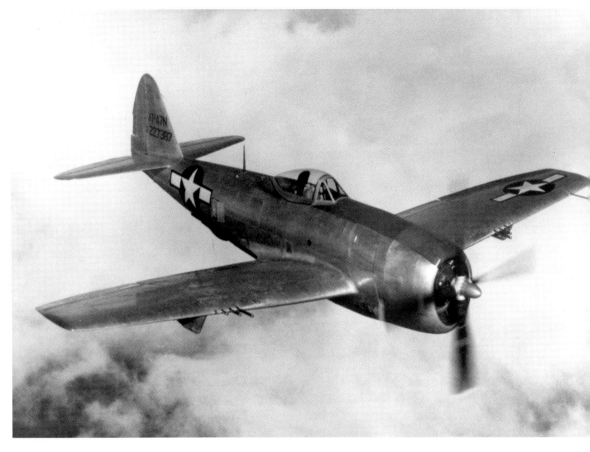

P-47 Thunderbolt fighter-bomber. The ubiquitous P-47s provided close air support to the 4th Armored Division during the fighting at Arracourt.

A knocked-out Panther from the 113th Panzer Brigade. This tank was destroyed by American fire as the American forward elements moved north toward Parroy.

they attempt to flank CCA headquarters from the northeast. The platoon, led by Lieutenant Leiper, deployed four of its M18 Hellcats forward as they reached Hill 246. As the M18s established their positions, Lieutenant Leiper spied an enemy tank emerging from the woods at the base of the hill.

As one postwar analysis recalled:

> The lead tank destroyer, commanded by Sgt. Stacey, had evidently seen the German tank at the same time as Lt. Leiper, and opened fire immediately. Its first round scored a direct hit, exploding the German tank. The flames of the burning tank revealed others behind it in a V-formation and Sgt. Stacy's next round hit the second German tank. But immediately afterwards, he had his own tank destroyer knocked out by fire from a third German tank. This enemy Mark IV [Panzer IV] was taken under fire by the number two tank destroyer and was destroyed. The maneuver and fire of the third tank destroyer got another German tank as it tried to back out of this unhealthy situation, and a fifth was destroyed almost immediately thereafter.

Sergeant Stacy's M18 sustained a direct hit in the front hull, killing the assistant driver and injuring the rest of the crew. The Hellcat itself, however, remained operational and returned to CCA headquarters under its own power. The three remaining tank destroyers withdrew to

Although the Panther tank packed more punch than the Sherman, its mechanical reliability was comparatively lower. The Panther was, in many ways, a victim of its over-engineered design. The interlaced road wheels offered a smoother ride, but maintenance was tough. Also, the transmission and final drives were problematic. The oncoming Allies were surprised to find that many of the abandoned Panthers they came across were non-functional due to faulty transmissions and other mechanical problems.

Three French boys inspect the charred remains of a German Panther. Although the Panther was well suited for standoff engagements, it fared poorly in close-quarters combat against the Sherman and its stablemates.

Major Charles Carpenter and his L-4H liaison plane. The industrious Carpenter modified the plane to accommodate a battery of bazookas that he could use for impromptu ground attacks. He thus christened his plane "Rosie the Rocketeer." Carpenter himself soon earned the nickname "Bazooka Charlie."

another nearby hill, whereupon they fired on another column of Panzer IV tanks, destroying at least four.

Meanwhile, from the air, Major Charles Carpenter was circling the battlefield aboard his L-4H liaison aircraft. Carpenter was the 4th Armored Division's forward aerial observer who had earned a reputation for his harrowing bravery and unorthodox techniques. For example, he had affixed a set of three 2.36-inch bazookas to the wings of his aircraft to facilitate attacking enemy ground troops. He thus named his aircraft "Rosie the Rocketeer," and Carpenter himself had earned the nickname "Bazooka Charlie." As Leiper's platoon fired on the enemy tanks, Carpenter noticed several more panzers trying to maneuver to the rear of Leiper's position. Carpenter then fired his airborne bazooka rounds in their direction, alerting Leiper's men of the incoming panzers to their rear.

Leiper directed another one of his tank destroyers to the rear, whereupon it killed two panzers before being immobilized by a hit to its right sprocket. Leiper then directed another M18 to recover the immobilized comrade. While attempting the recovery, however, that M18 also was hit by a lingering panzer, destroying the Hellcat and its crew. Leiper then withdrew his one remaining tank destroyer.

Hearing this melee unfold over the radio, Creighton Abrams dispatched a section of three M4s to support Leiper's tank destroyers, but one of these incoming Shermans was hit by a Panzerfaust while engaging enemy dismounts. Leiper's sole surviving M18 was then directed to join 2d Platoon, Company C, 704th Tank Destroyer Battalion as they set up defenses on the high ground between Arracourt and Athienville. The move was fortuitous as they were soon greeted by a company-sized element of 14 German tanks. In a quick, rapid-fire engagement, the Hellcats destroyed eight tanks, forcing the rest of the enemy column into retreat.

An analysis of the German tanks that fought in and around Arracourt reveals some surprising data. German tanks didn't seem to be qualitatively better built; they simply had different tradeoffs than the American tanks. For example, the Panther had strong frontal armor, but worse gas mileage. The Panzer IV had similar performance metrics to the M4 Sherman, but its reliability lagged behind the Sherman after comparable field hours.

Task Force Hunter, having just returned from its defense of Lunéville, took Companies A and B of the 37th Tank Battalion and swept through the area east of Arracourt to neutralize any remaining German tanks. Resistance was piecemeal at this point, but the two companies collectively registered eight destroyed enemy tanks and nearly 100 enemy dismounts killed. By this time, Patton, Eddy, and Wood (4th Armored Division commander) could see that the Wehrmacht was against the ropes. Although Wood's division had been stretched pretty thin, Patton concluded that his combat assets had the wherewithal to continue the attack. Patton thus ordered the "Name Enough" Division to continue its advance to the River Saar the next day.

*

By the morning of September 20, CCA had been heavily reinforced to affect its drive to the German border. Their attachments included the 35th and 37th Tank Battalions, two armored infantry battalions, and three field artillery battalions. Although the Germans had entered the fight at Arracourt with strength in numbers, their losses over the course of September 19/20 had diminished their forces to a fraction of what they needed to be "combat effective." By some estimates, their force ratios had fallen to as little as 4:1 in favor of the Americans. Manteuffel's subordinate corps commander insisted that a counterattack against the 4th Armored Division was no longer feasible given the attrition of his own units. But Manteuffel, perhaps reluctantly, ordered his panzer units to continue the attack.

For the September 20 operation, the 111th Panzer Brigade was selected to lead the attack through Arracourt. If the 111th could not sustain the momentum, the Germans' contingency plan was to draw the Americans back towards the Marne–Rhine Canal, where a regiment of Flakpanzers would open fire alongside the 113th Panzer Brigade.

On the morning of September 20, CCA moved out of its assembly areas, whereupon they once again encountered the recurring fog and rain. At around 11:00 AM, the first enemy rounds of the day landed near CCA's command post, courtesy of the 111th Panzer Brigade. The 191st Field Artillery returned the favor with a volley from their 155mm howitzers. Their fire mission, however, was against incoming tanks at less than 200 yards—essentially point-blank range in the world of artillery. The fusillade was enough to disable two enemy tanks, whereupon the remaining panzers withdrew. That day, American artillery was credited with killing six enemy tanks.

At approximately 11:30, the 35th and 37th Tank Battalions maneuvered to destroy any remaining German tanks in the area. Creighton Abrams's 37th Tank Battalion, however, took the lion's share of the action that day. While heading towards Ley, elements of Company C ran into a German ambush consisting of seven tanks and multiple PaK 40 antitank guns. The Americans lost six M4 Shermans during the melee but accounted for all seven enemy tanks and a handful of PaK 40s destroyed.

In Profile:
The 37th Tank Battalion

One of the most famed armored units of World War II, the 37th Tank Battalion prided themselves as being the "first in Bastogne," during the time of the infamous Battle of the Bulge. Later that spring, the 37th Tank Battalion helped liberate an American POW camp near Himmelberg. The battalion's commanding officer was Creighton "Abe" Abrams, one of the leading minds in American armored warfare.

Patton once said of Abrams: "I'm supposed to be the best tank commander in the army, but I have one peer—Abe Abrams. He's the world champion." Abrams went on to command American forces in Vietnam, and later served as Chief of Staff of the Army from 1972–4. He was the only Chief of Staff to die in office, succumbing to complications following surgery to remove a cancerous lung.

Two Shermans from the 37th Tank Battalion in Germany, March 1945.

An M5A1 Stuart from the 25th Cavalry Squadron, knocked out by a German Panther during the opening rounds of the fighting near Juvelize.

A knocked-out Sherman gives mute evidence of the casualties suffered by the 4th Armored Division in its drive to the German borderlands.

Mounted aboard a Sherman tank, these American crews spot the impact of a nearby Allied artillery round. Howitzer artillery (and its associated fire support assets) was the one combat arm wherein the Americans had unparalleled superiority over the Wehrmacht.

Later that evening, a company from the 10th Armored Infantry Battalion along with an M4 Sherman company from the 37th attacked a forward position of the 113th Panzer Brigade at Moncourt. The 37th Tank Battalion logs recounted the nighttime battle as such:

Night was falling, and from the battalion CP [command post] area, the glow of burning Ley began to light up the sky. Despite gathering darkness, the order was still "attack." The attack against Moncourt, executed at night, was a new departure from the "book" which said that tanks could not be successfully employed in the dark. Preceding the attack, the artillery laid a preparatory fire on Moncourt. The attack on Moncourt was delivered from the west of the Ley–Moncourt Road, which was the general line of advance. In a tight and intermingled formation, three tank companies and two infantry companies approached Moncourt. The whole formation opened fire as one, presenting an awesome sight, and the storm of incendiary bullets and high explosive set Moncourt afire as the forces moved in, grinding the opposition outside the town. All this this was in complete contradiction to the German conception that Americans never attack at night, and always stick to roads. Lt. Donnelly's A Company platoon then went into the town with A Company of the 10th [Armored Infantry Battalion]. The infantry used bayonets, grenades and submachine guns and rifles, slaughtering the Germans in their foxholes where they were immobilized by fear and the shock of the assault.

A destroyed Panzer IV north of Juvelize. From the relative position of its turret, this panzer was likely destroyed by a P-47 Thunderbolt.

By the end of the night on September 20, Creighton Abrams's battalion claimed 16 enemy tanks and more than 250 enemy killed. German records for the 19th and 20th of September are nondescript, but in some places, they confirm losing 11 panzers while claiming 18 Shermans destroyed.

Blaskowitz, the Army Group G commander, and Manteuffel were understandably upset by the lack of progress from the 5th Panzer Army. But their frustrations were the least of their worries—Adolf Hitler was livid and he was determined to make an example out of someone. He fired Blaskowitz on September 20 and replaced him with General Hermann Balck.

*

September 21 passed without incident for both the 4th Armored Division and their German counterparts. At the higher echelons, Patton was discussing the logistical needs for continuing operations while Manteuffel was awaiting orders from his new boss. Thus, September 21 became a day of rest, maintenance, and recuperation.

During the lull, however, the 11th Panzer Division arrived at the front, bringing 10 new Panthers and 20 Panzer IVs, though many were no longer operational. But despite the dire situation, morale was high; the division was perhaps the most experienced combat unit entering the 5th Panzer Army's ranks. Moreover, the division had received an additional 2,000 troops—involuntary transfers from the Luftwaffe. For the forthcoming operations,

A pair of tanks from the 11th Panzer Division, in Dieuze, northeast of Arracourt. September 23, 1944.

the 111th Panzer Brigade was attached to the division, which added 30 more tanks, but here again, few were operational.

The Germans' objective for September 22 was to halt the 4th Armored Division's advance from Arracourt into Lezey and beyond. The German 1st Army was supposed to send the 553d Volksgrenadier Division and 17th SS Panzergrenadier Division as supporting elements, but neither unit arrived in time for the September 22 operation. The battle plan was to envelope CCA's forward elements (including the 37th Tank Battalion) in a semi-pincer movement. The 11th Panzer Division and the 111th Panzer Brigade would attack from the north, while the 113th Panzer Brigade would attack from the south.

First contact occurred shortly after 9:00 AM when the panzergrneadiers encountered the forward outposts of the 25th Cavalry near Hill 252. During the opening volleys, a platoon of M5 Stuarts came to assist the cavalry scouts, but the entire platoon was cut down by a Panther company that emerged from the fog. As the cavalrymen withdrew from the area, however, a nearby section of M18 Hellcats sallied forward to interdict the oncoming Panthers. The lead M18 knocked out three Panther tanks before withdrawing with the cavalry scouts.

As reports from the cavalry screen line flowed back into Creighton Abrams's headquarters, he ordered his battalion into action. Company C rode forward to assist the

A pair of tanks from Combat Command B move through a field of dead cattle while supporting the 35th Infantry Division near Chateau Salinas on September 22, 1944.

Colonel von Seckendorf, commander of the 113th Panzer Brigade. Von Seckendorf was killed in action during the battle of Arracourt, the victim of a P-47 Thunderbolt attack. His counterpart, the commander of the 111th Panzer Brigade, was also killed during the battle, cut down by machine-gun fire as he dismounted his halftrack.

retreating cavalrymen while covering the westward approach from the Lezey–Juvelize road. By 10:00 AM, however, the fog had lifted and the 37th Tank Battalion saw the return of an old friend—P-47 Thunderbolts from the local air support squadron. Now that visibility was clear, the P-47s strafed and bombed the incoming panzers and truck-mounted panzergrenadiers.

Company A, meanwhile, occupied positions near Juvelize proper to prevent any German flanking movements from the south. An M3 halftrack company attached from the 10th Armored Infantry Battalion joined Company A as they set up their blocking positions. But because German troops had already set up inside Juvelize proper, Abrams ordered an artillery and mortar strike on the town as "covering fire" ahead of Company A's movement. With a screen of white phosphorus and high-explosive rounds, Company A was unmolested by enemy fire as it established its blocking positions. As Company A settled into position, however, a spotter aircraft detected more enemy tanks in the area. Abrams then ordered Company C to tie in with Company A's left flank. These reinforcements were a welcomed addition, as Company A was down to only two platoons after sustaining heavy casualties over the previous days' fighting.

As the enemy tanks moved into Company A's kill zone, both platoons opened fire, engaging German tanks at rounds of 400 to 2,000 yards. When the smoke cleared, Company A had accounted for 14 enemy tanks, including an M5 Stuart that the Germans had captured earlier that day (presumably during the 25th Cavalry's retreat from Hill 252). Having halted the Germans' attempt to reinforce Juvelize, Abrams then created a small task force consisting of a tank platoon from Company B and a motorized infantry platoon from the 10th Armored Infantry Battalion. He instructed this combined-arms task force to clear Juvelize of all enemy forces. The tank–infantry team accomplished its task with zeal, destroying all remnants of the 211th Panzergrenadier Regiment inside Juvelize.

The two local panzer brigades tried to organize a counterattack, but to no avail—they were beaten back by American artillery and the roving P-47 patrols. In fact, the commanding

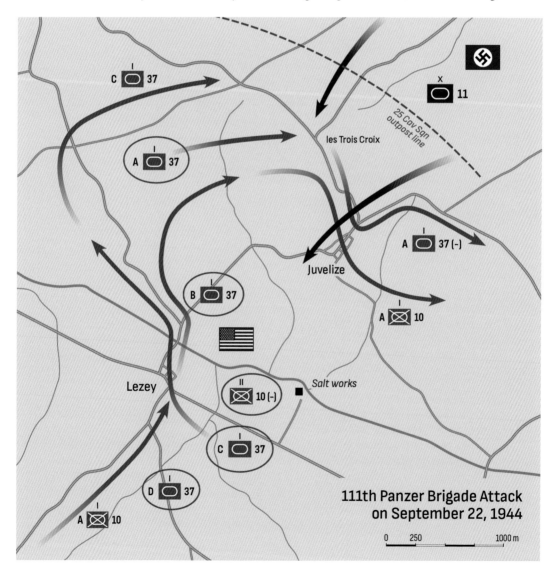

les Trois Croix

25 Cav Sqn outpost line

Juvelize

Lezey

Salt works

111th Panzer Brigade Attack
on September 22, 1944

0   250   1000 m

A medic tends to a wounded soldier from the 37th Tank Battalion north of Arracourt, September 24.

officers of both panzer brigades were killed during the fighting. The 111th Panzer Brigade commander, Colonel Heinrich von Bronsant-Schellendorf, was killed by machine-gun fire after dismounting his halftrack. However, some of his subordinate officers felt that he had purposely exposed himself to enemy fire, hoping to be killed as a means to escape an unwinnable situation. The commander of the 113th Panzer Brigade, meanwhile, was killed during a surprise attack from a P-47. Both officers were posthumously promoted from colonel to general.

By nightfall on September 22, the 111th Panzer Brigade had been reduced to only seven tanks from its original strength of ninety. Throughout the day, they had lost an additional 250 men. Losses in the 4th Armored Division were comparatively light—eight tanks destroyed, and seven soldiers killed.

Contributing to the German defeat at Arracourt, and during much of the last year of the war, was the constant shakeup of senior Wehrmacht officers and micromanagement from Hitler himself. Following the failed assassination attempt in July 1944, the Führer became evermore distrustful of the generals and field marshals along the Western Front. He applied pressure to men like Blaskowitz and Manteuffel for results, even though he realized they didn't have the sufficient force structure or resources to accomplish the goals. Moreover, fighting a war on two fronts had stretched the German war machine beyond its capacity to fight effectively.

A despairing Manteuffel, meanwhile, consolidated what was left of his panzer brigades into the neighboring divisions. After three days of fighting (September 19–22), the 111th and 113th Panzer Brigades were virtually in shambles. During that same time, Combat Command A had lost only 14 Shermans and seven M5 Stuarts.

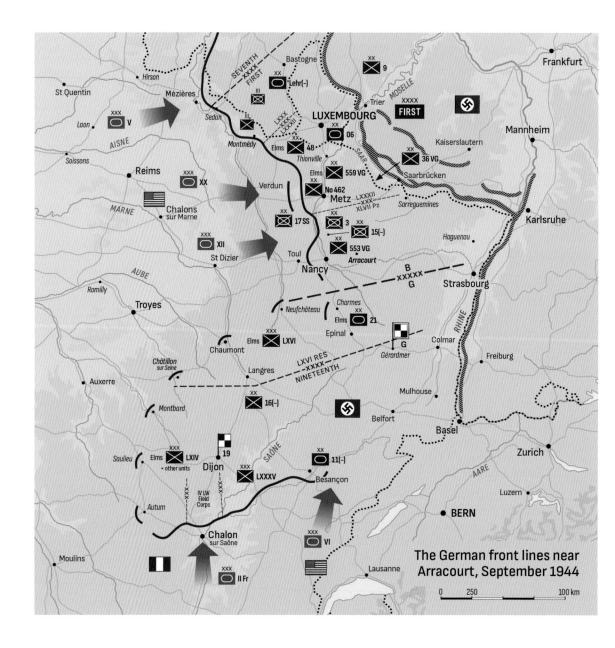

The German front lines near Arracourt, September 1944

0   250   100 km

The Vosges panzer offensive had failed.

But during the final week of September, the battered German 1st Army and 5th Panzer Army would make one final effort to stop the Allies from reaching the German border.

*

By September 24, Hitler knew that the strategic situation in France was rapidly deteriorating. By the time the panzer battles in Arracourt had begun, the Allies had already launched Operation *Market Garden*, an entire American corps had entered Belgium, and the U.S. 3d

Armored Division was barreling towards the German city of Aachen. Hitler thus diverted most of his resources to support these areas, but nonetheless allowed the 11th Panzer Division to reinforce the ailing units in Lorraine.

Patton, meanwhile, was forced to take up defensive positions due to (a) the continuing shortage of supplies, and (b) the fact that he would soon be losing the 6th Armored Division and XV Corps to facilitate the drive to the Rhine. But while Patton set up his defenses, General Balck of Army Group G devised a new counteroffensive. In the 1st Army sector, the 559th Volksgrenadier Division would attack west towards Moncel-sur-Seille, supported by remnants of the 106th Panzer Brigade. The 5th Panzer Army would then link up with 1st Army elements, forming a line against the 4th Armored Division.

The fighting on September 24 began around 5:00 AM in the 1st Army sector near Chateau Salinas. Unlike the previous attacks, this counteroffensive began with a well-coordinated artillery strike. Indeed the 559th Volksgrenadier Division had a full contingent of artillery whereas the panzer brigades had none. The forward scouts of Combat Command B detected the incoming fire and called on the local artillery units for counterbattery fire. As the incoming wave of German infantry arrived on the field, American artillery helped repel the attack. By 10:00 AM, the P-47s had once again taken to the sky, strafing enemy positions from altitudes as low as 15 feet. Within the next 15 minutes, the 559th Volksgrenadier Division collapsed.

This tank from 2d Platoon, Company C, 37th Tank Battalion was the only tank in its platoon to survive the fighting at Arracourt from September 19–25. This photo was taken south of Parroy around September 26.

Lieutenant James Fields was awarded the Medal of Honor for heroism as a member of Company A, 10th Armored Infantry Battalion.

After some touch-and-go engagements on September 25, CCA and CCB took up defensive positions in keeping with Patton's new orders. But the German attacks resumed on September 27, this time with 24 Panthers, six Panzer IVs, and a handful of StuG III assault guns. A weary Manteuffel ordered the 11th Panzer Division (including remnants of the 113th Panzer Brigade) to attack towards Arracourt.

Company A from the 10th Armored Infantry Battalion bore the brunt of the attack along its hilltop outposts near Rechicourt. A report from the neighboring 51st Armored Infantry Battalion described the action as follows:

> Company A's position in Rechicourt became the focal point for enemy artillery. Concentrations consisted of 105s and heavier. The road through town became known as the "Bowling Alley" as it was obviously under enemy observation and more than one vehicle in any one spot immediately brought artillery fire.

But there was no shortage of valor in Company A's sector. One platoon leader, Lieutenant James Fields, distinguished himself during an attack on an enemy position. Although wounded by a shellburst that cut his teeth, gums, nasal cavity, and temporarily robbed him of his speech, he refused to be evacuated and continued directing his platoon through hand and arm signals. At one point, he took out two enemy machine-gun nests, destroying both, and saving his platoon from a deadly crossfire.

When Fields was finally evacuated, another lieutenant from nearby Company C took over his platoon. Within moments of his arrival, however, the platoon began taking fire from a German tank some 150 yards away. Small-arms fire killed the exposed panzer commander, but the tank itself remained operational and took defilade while returning fire on the American dismounts. The new lieutenant called on the local tank destroyers for assistance but, for reasons unknown, the M18s refused the call. Seeing that his platoon's situation was untenable, the lieutenant had his men fall back towards Rechicourt.

Dismounts from the 10th Armored Infantry Battalion. Aside from its token tank battalions, the 4th Armored Division had a number of armored infantry battalions, comparable to today's mechanized infantry.

Company C, meanwhile, stayed busy defending Hill 265. Reinforced by a platoon of M18s, Company C spent most of September 26 and 27 beating back assaults from the 110th Panzergrenadier Regiment. The panzergrenadiers then attempted a similar assault on the 51st Armored Infantry Battalion and gained ground against the Americans on Hill 318. By noon on September 28, however, the Germans had been beaten back off the hill. Later that night, and into the predawn hours, the ailing Germans sent numerous probing patrols into the American lines, looking for weaknesses to exploit. Each of their patrols, however, were promptly cut down by the 25th Cavalry's screen line.

The Germans made their final push for Arracourt on the morning of September 29, 1944. For this last-ditch effort, the 11th Panzer Division consolidated every piece of armor they had left. Massing opposite from Combat Command B, the Germans gathered 20 Panther tanks, 18 Panzer IVs, and 11 Flakpanzer IV guns. However, only a small percentage of these vehicles remained functional.

The U.S. 8th Tank Battalion, which had been sent forward to assist the 51st Armored Infantry Battalion, made first contact with this renewed German attack at 11:00 AM, taking heavy mortar fire. One of the tank company commanders radioed for air support; throughout the day, the P-47s once again appeared over the skies, strafing German positions and driving them into the kill zones of American artillery. The German vehicles not yet destroyed by the air and artillery strikes were now being cut down by Company C from the 8th Tank Battalion. The carnage was so severe that even the 11th Panzer Division commander took notice:

In a few minutes, 18 of our tanks and several armored personnel carriers were burning! Our own infantry retreated, strangely enough not pursued by the enemy. *As a result, any chance of winning our final objective had been frustrated* [emphasis added]. We had suffered losses that could have been prevented if only we had been satisfied with the line already gained, which was suitable for the defense.

By mid-afternoon, the Germans were in full retreat. By now, the 5th Panzer Army had been reduced to barely a handful of tanks. Moreover, they had lost more than 700 men killed and 300 wounded. After three days of unsuccessful counterattacks, the 5th Panzer Army quit the field and withdrew towards the German frontier. Their last attempts to halt the Third Army's advance to the German border had failed.

The battle of Arracourt was over. The 4th Armored Division had won.

Soldiers from the 53d Armored Infantry Battalion, 4th Armored Division prepare to move to the front. Note the body of their fallen comrade in the foreground, carefully prepared on a stretcher for the oncoming mortuary affairs handlers.

| Afterword

Some historians have characterized the Lorraine campaign as a stalemate, pointing to the fact that supply shortages forced Patton into a defensive position, and the panzer forces were exhausted, depleted, and incapable of mounting any further offensives. This assessment, however, misses the bigger picture—namely, that the Allies—and the U.S. Third Army in particular—gained much of the ground that they wanted.

By the standards of attritional warfare, the 4th Armored Division commanded the kill/loss ratio by a sizable margin. In one engagement after another (ranging from the platoon level to battalion level), the Americans had bested the German 1st Army and 5th Panzer Army in convincing fashion.

Indeed, of the 262 German tanks and assault guns at Arracourt, 200 were destroyed or were rendered combat ineffective. The 4th Armored Division, on the other hand, fared much better. Combat Command A, which had done most of the fighting at Arracourt, lost

A knocked-out Panther from the 11th Panzer Division in the northern sector of Arracourt. Following the battle of Arracourt, the division withdrew from the area and participated in the Battle of the Bulge, then shifted to the Ruhr before surrendering to Allied forces on May 2, 1945.

After their defeat at Arracourt, the 5th Panzer Army withdrew and regrouped for the Ardennes offensive. However, Manteuffel and his forces were routed near Bastogne, with much of their equipment destroyed by the U.S. 2d Armored Division. Here lies the charred remains an abandoned Panzer IV (foreground) and Panther tank (background) from the 5th Panzer Army.

only 25 tanks and seven M18 tank destroyers. The division as a whole lost some 50 tanks (including M4s and M5s) throughout September.

Examining the battle from a tactical and technical perspective, one sees a glaring difference in the training, crew proficiency, and comparative combat power between the U.S. Army and the Wehrmacht. To be fair, the Panther tank had a technological edge over the Sherman in terms of armored protection and punching power, but a combination of poor maintenance and crew training eroded much of the Panther's advantages. In fact, German tanks in the ETO performed better against American armor when operating from defensive positions. Most tanks have a natural advantage when operating from the defense; and the kills scored from these defensive postures may have contributed to the ongoing myth of German armor's unilateral superiority. When reviewing the engagement data, however, one sees that American tanks also produced more kills when operating from defensive postures. During offensive operations, however, when both American and German armor were maneuvering against each other, German kill ratios fell precipitously. In these instances, it was clear that American tactics won the day even though the Panthers had superior metrics in armor and firepower. The Americans also had a decided advantage in artillery and air support. American forward observers and air liaisons had better communications capability than did the Wehrmacht, as well as the means to keep pace with their armored formations. Moreover, by the fall of 1944, the Luftwaffe was no longer effective as an aerial support arm.

When analyzing the comparative losses in equipment during September 1944, it's clear that most of the American tank casualties were caused by antitank guns, not enemy tanks. From a higher-level view, the U.S. Army in Lorraine achieved a kill/loss ratio of 2.4 to 1 over the Wehrmacht. During the battle of Arracourt itself, the 4th Armored Division's kill/loss ratio stood even higher—nearly 4 to 1. This stands as a testament not so much to the Sherman itself, but to the audacious crews who manned them, and the fire support teams who assisted them.

Technical and tactical analyses aside, there is little doubt that the battle of Arracourt had a significant impact for both Axis and Allies. In the first sustained tank-on-tank battle of the Western Front, the burgeoning M4 Sherman units proved their mettle against a battle-hardened enemy with a formidable fleet of panzers. The destruction of their panzer units in and around Arracourt forced the Germans to reevaluate both their tactics *and* their overall defensive strategy for the German frontier. But by the fall of 1944, the damage had been done. The collapse of the Vosges panzer offensive, and the defeat at Arracourt, paved the way for the Allied advance across the River Saar and into the industrial heartland of the Reich. A mere seven months later, Nazi Germany surrendered and the war in Europe came to an end.

| Further Reading

Barnes, Richard. *Arracourt: September 1944*. Auckland: Lucknow Books, 1983.

Cameron, Robert S. *Mobility, Shock, and Firepower: The Emergence of the U.S. Army's Armor Branch, 1917–1945*. Washington DC: U.S. Government Printing Office, 2008.

Colby, John. *War from the Ground Up: The 90th Division in World War II*. Austin: Nortex, 1991.

Cole, Hugh. *The Lorraine Campaign*. Washington DC: U.S. Army Center for Military History, 1981.

Cooper, Belton. *Death Traps: The Survival of an American Armored Division in World War II*. Novato: Presidio Press, 1998.

Gabel, Christopher. *The 4th Armored Division in the Encirclement of Nancy*. Auckland: Lucknow Books, 1986.

Hofmann, George F., & Donn A. Starry. *Camp Colt to Desert Storm: The History of U.S. Armored Forces*. Lexington: University Press of Kentucky, 2013.

Yeide, Harry. *The Infantry's Armor: The U.S. Army's Separate Tank Battalions in World War II*. Mechanicsville: Stackpole Books, 2010.

Zaloga, Steve. *Armored Thunderbolt: The U.S. Army Sherman in World War II*. Mechanicsville: Stackpole Books, 2008.

Zaloga, Steve. *Lorraine 1944: Patton vs. Mateuffel*. London: Bloomsbury Publishing, 2000.

Zaloga, Steven J. *Patton versus the Panzers: The Battle of Arracourt, September 1944*. London: Bloomsbury Publishing, 2016.

| Index

1st Army (German), 6, 8, 13, 54–5, 57,
   63, 71, 73, 79, 112, 116–17, 121
5th Panzer Army, 6–8, 13, 39, 54, 56–7,
   59–63, 65–6, 71, 73, 78–9, 87, 90, 97,
   100–11, 116–17, 120–1, 123

Aachen, 117
Abrams, Creighton, 13, 35, 80, 89, 100,
   105–7, 111–14
Armored Division
   4th, 6–8, 13, 17–18, 25, 29–31, 34–6,
      39, 44, 50, 59, 68, 71, 77–80, 84–5,
      87–8, 90, 93, 97, 100, 103, 105–6,
      109, 111–12, 115, 117, 119–21, 124
   6th, 30–1, 97, 117
   7th, 30, 75
Armored Infantry Battalion
   10th, 7, 31, 87, 110, 113–14, 118–19
   51st, 31, 118–19
   53d, 31, 93, 120
Army Group G, 55–6, 58–9, 63, 66, 87,
   97, 111, 117
Arracourt, 6–9, 14, 17, 22, 26, 30, 34, 36,
   39–40, 42, 44, 50, 54–5, 59, 63, 66, 71,
   77–8, 81, 85, 88–94, 96–8, 100, 102–3,
   105–6, 111–13, 115–21, 123–4
Athienville, 105
Atlantic Wall, 54, 56, 71

Balck, Hermann, 111, 117
Bayon Canal, 77–9
Berlin, 97
Blaskowitz, Johannes, 55, 87, 111, 115
Bradley, Omar, 36, 66

Caen, 41, 66, 71
Carpenter, Charlie, 105
Cavalry Squadron
   25th, 25, 31, 39, 100, 108, 112, 114, 119
   42d, 85, 87–8
Chambois, 71
Chateau Salinas, 112, 117

Combat Commands, 7, 30–1, 34, 36,
   77–80, 84, 87–8, 112, 115, 117, 119, 121

Dieulouard, 50, 77–8, 80

Eastern Front, 41–2, 44, 49–50, 62, 65,
   74, 97
Eddy, Manton, 29, 77, 79, 106
Epinal, 75

Falaise Pocket, 62, 71
Field Artillery Battalion,
   22d, 31
   66th, 31
   94th, 31, 93, 100
   191st, 34, 98, 106
Fields, James, 118
Flakpanzer IV, 50–1, 54, 119
Forêt de Mondon, 87
Forêt de Parroy, 87

Guderian, Heinz, 49, 62, 82

Hill 252, 112, 114
Hill 265, 7, 119
Hitler, Adolf, 6–9, 42, 48, 50, 54–5, 57, 59,
   62, 71, 73, 79–80, 85, 87, 111, 115–17

Infantry Division
   35th, 77, 79, 112
   80th, 50, 77, 80
   90th, 67, 69, 74

Jagdpanzer IV, 41, 49–50
Juvelize, 108, 110, 113–14

Lend-Lease Program, 8, 12, 23
Lezey, 100, 112–13
Lorraine, 6–7, 37, 55, 57, 59, 61–2, 64, 71,
   74, 77, 81, 83–4, 117, 121, 124
Luftwaffe, 50, 57, 64, 71, 73, 84, 111, 124
Lunéville, 7, 28, 46, 80, 85–8, 90, 93, 97, 106

M3 Halftrack, 8, 14–15, 19–21, 27–8, 34, 39, 47–8, 113

M3/M5 Stuart, 14–15, 21, 34, 100, 108, 112, 114–15

M4 Sherman, 7–8, 12, 14–15, 17–19, 21, 27, 34, 39–40, 43, 50, 67–8, 75, 78, 81–2, 84, 87–8, 95, 102, 104–6, 109–11, 115, 124

M7 Howitzer Motor Carriage, 21–22, 34, 88

M8 Greyhound Light Armored Car, 14, 22–5, 39, 80, 85, 88

M18 Hellcat, 27–8, 39–40, 88–90, 104–5, 112, 118–19, 124

Metz, 73, 82, 100

Moselle River, 7, 54–5, 69, 71–3, 75, 77, 80, 87

Normandy, 6, 8, 11–14, 28, 30, 36, 39, 41, 50, 54–5, 57, 62–3, 66–7, 71, 74–5, 82

Ommeray, 100

Operation *Cobra*, 37, 39, 67–8

Operation *Market Garden*, 116

Operation *Thunderbolt*, 77

P-47 Thunderbolt, 71, 103, 110, 113–15, 117, 119

Panther tank, 8, 14, 19, 36–7, 40–4, 49, 59, 62–4, 66, 68, 75, 81–2, 84, 88, 90–4, 96, 100–4, 106, 108, 111–12, 118–19, 121, 123–4

Panzer Brigade
106th, 57–8, 73–5, 117
111th, 7, 46, 59–60, 62, 86–8, 90–3, 96–7, 100–1, 106, 112–13, 115
112th, 59–60, 62
113th, 7, 59–60, 62, 93, 100, 102–3, 106, 110, 112–13, 115, 118

Panzer Division
11th, 57, 62fn, 66, 111–12, 117–19, 121
21st, 57, 62–3, 87

Panzer IV, 8, 14, 19, 40–4, 47, 49–50, 57, 59, 78, 81–2, 84, 86, 90, 100, 104–6, 110–11, 118–19, 123

Panzergrenadier Division
3d, 57, 77–8
15th, 7, 57, 71, 73, 78–9, 87, 90
17th SS, 57, 68, 75, 112

Patton, George, 7–9, 18, 23, 26, 29–30, 34, 36, 39, 55, 59–60, 65–6, 71, 73, 75, 77, 85, 95, 97, 100, 106–7, 111, 117–18, 121

Rechicourt, 94, 102, 118, 120

Rhine River, 8, 71, 75, 106, 117

"Rosie the Rocketeer," 105

Saar River, 7, 97, 106, 124

Sd.Kfz. halftrack, 37, 47–8, 57–8, 61, 70, 75, 87, 101

StuG III assault gun, 45–7, 49–50, 67, 77, 80, 118

Tank Battalion
8th, 18–19, 31, 39, 77, 87, 119
35th, 31, 80, 87–8, 106
37th, 7, 17, 31, 35, 80, 93, 95, 100, 102, 106–7, 110, 112–13, 115, 117

tank destroyers, 19, 22, 27–8, 30, 35, 39–40, 45, 48–50, 57, 67, 74, 88, 102, 104–5, 118, 124

Task Force Hunter, 90, 97, 106

(U.S.) Third Army, 6–9, 23, 26, 29–30, 34, 37, 39, 55, 59–60, 66, 68, 71, 73–5, 79, 97, 120–1

Volksgrenadier Division
19th, 57, 73
36th, 57
462d, 57
559th, 57, 69, 117, 65, 85, 87, 93, 97, 100, 106, 111, 115, 118, 123

von Manteuffel, Hasso, 56, 60

Vosges panzer offensive, 7, 71–3, 75, 80, 85, 116, 124

Wehrmacht, 8–9, 12, 14, 19, 29, 40–1, 43, 45, 47–50, 54, 57–9, 62–4, 67, 71, 75, 78, 81, 84, 106, 115, 124

Westwall, 71

Wood, John S., 29, 36, 80, 88, 95

Other Titles in the Casemate Illustrated Series:

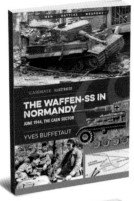

THE WAFFEN-SS IN NORMANDY: JUNE 1944, THE CAEN SECTOR

by Yves Buffetaut

Follows how the Waffen-SS fared in Normandy during June 1944 and whether they deserved their reputation of being the ultimate fighting soldiers.
OCTOBER 2018 | 9781612006055

ALLIED ARMOR IN NORMANDY

by Yves Buffetaut

Explores the Normandy invasion from the perspective of the Allied Armored divisions, looking at how armored vehicles played a central role in the many battles that took place.
JUNE 2018 | 9781612006079

THE FALAISE POCKET: NORMANDY, AUGUST 1944

by Yves Buffetaut

A highly illustrated account of the battle of the Falaise Pocket, Normandy 1944.
APRIL 2019 | 9781612007274

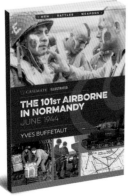

THE 101st AIRBORNE IN NORMANDY: JUNE 1944

by Yves Buffetaut

This fully illustrated volume examines the actions of the 101st in Normandy.
APRIL 2018 | 9781612005232